Love at the
Last Minute

Rhonda Hayes Curtis

For more information, go to www.rhondahayescurtis.com

Cover Design by: Scarlett Rugers
Interior Design by: The Write Assistants
Bio Photo by: Brad Smith

Love at the Last Minute / Rhonda Hayes Curtis —1st ed.

ISBN 978-0-9971470-0-1

Praise for Love at the Last Minute

"With deft, simple strokes, Rhonda Hayes Curtis paints a beautiful panorama of love, loss, and second chances that honors and celebrates both the sweetness and sorrow of life. At once heartwarming and heartbreaking, this moving memoir reassures us that even in the darkest of times, life will do its best to bring us blessings to ease our pain."

- Phil Bolsta, author of *Through God's Eyes: Finding Peace and Purpose in a Troubled World*

"This is a beautiful memoir, heart wrenching in so many ways and yet filled with hope. But at its heart this is a love story, a reminder that in the end there's nothing more powerful than two people caring for each other."

- Evan Miller, senior editor, *Guideposts* magazine

"*Love at the Last Minute* is a deeply moving ride through the ever shifting landscape of life, loss and love. While on one of the bumpiest roads of life, Rhonda Hayes Curtis eloquently shares the blessings of being fully present to desperate hope, trust in a daughter's most unusual request, crushing grief, surrender and the tenderness of love. An awe inspiring read!"

- Gail D. Gerbie, Licensed Marriage and Family Therapist

"Rhonda Hayes Curtis takes us on a bittersweet journey that captivates the reader as she learns to accept tragic losses with grace, and receive unexpected love with an open heart. A sincere and honest account of life's complexity and richness."

- Carol Ann Haines, author of *Living Fit after Fifty: A Guide for the Post-Menopausal Woman.*

"*Love at the Last Minute* is a poignant and inspiring memoir of a mother, facing every mother's worst nightmare – the loss of a child, and the incredible gift of love her daughter leaves behind. With a remarkably brave and open heart, Hayes Curtis gently reminds us that we hold the key to healing our broken hearts after tragedy when we unlock the transformative power of our grief with the painful acceptance of life's unacceptable losses... and that love truly begets love."

- Lauri Taylor, author of *The Accidental Truth: What My Mother's Murder Investigation Taught Me About Life*

Table of Contents

Dedicated to

Larry, Charlotte, Lisa, and Gina

In Loving Memory of Greg and Sherry

Chapter One

Get a Life

I WAS MASSAGING SHERRY'S feet, imagining my fingertips releasing some kind of magical energy to cure her cancer, when she pressed "pause" on the TV remote. Our eyes met. She smiled. "Mom," she said, "you need to get a life."

A life? A few days earlier, the oncologist had sent her home from the hospital saying hospice was her best option. I smiled back. "Sweetie, you are my life."

"I know, Mom." She coughed. "I don't know what I'd do

without you."

I lowered my head and took a deep breath. In just two years, I'd seen so many changes in Sherry from the chemo—moon face, weight loss, hair loss, and rashes. Her once wispy hair had grown in thick and choppy. Fifteen pounds heavier, she looked different, but not like she was dying.

"What will you do when I'm gone?" She paused. "You need to move on."

My stomach tightened. Since my husband's funeral, nine months before, I had been spending five nights a week with Sherry and her husband Chris. But now I had just rented out my townhome and settled in to live full-time with them. *Why was she talking about moving on?* Now all that mattered was this time with her. I gently tugged at her toes, hoping we could get back to what our typical afternoons had come to be: sitting together in her family room, watching TV with her Yorkies, Rose and Olivia, curled up beside us.

But Sherry had more on her mind. Reaching for my hand, she said, "Mom, you know that's what Dad wanted. That's what I want."

During Greg's long illness, he'd told me he wanted me to find someone after he was gone, and I believed that I would someday. Several weeks earlier, while I was out walking the dogs, a list of qualities I would look for in a new mate popped into my head: Kind. Loving. Honest. I wanted to tell Sherry, but she was part of a clinical trial for a new chemo drug, so I decided to wait until we got the good news. The good news never came. How could I think about "getting a life" or anything else other than my daughter?

Suddenly, Sherry sat up. "A dating site. That's it!" she said, like she'd just solved a murder mystery.

A dating site? My heart pounded. I reached for the remote, turning my attention to the TV. Howie Mandel bumped his fists with a woman contestant. "Did you see that? He didn't shake her hand."

"You've never noticed that before?" Sherry always noticed details. She was meticulous about everything—the books on the shelf in alphabetical order, the Queen Anne chairs turned at the right angle, the kitchen desk neat and tidy. She continued, "He's a germaphobe."

"Really? How do you know that?" Anything to divert the subject away from me and dating. Greg hadn't even been gone a year. Wouldn't that be like cheating on him? We had been together for twenty-five years, since I was thirty.

When Sherry was diagnosed two years before, I promised to give her anything she wanted. I couldn't imagine what it might be—she was happy. She loved her husband, dogs, home, and career. I knew my daughter as well as any mother could. But if I was missing something, if she had any dreams or goals that I didn't know about, I wanted her to live them. If she was only pretending to be happy, I wanted to fix it. I wanted nothing but her happiness. So later that night in my room, I supposed I should at least try to do what she asked.

I opened my laptop, a Gateway that I'd bought before Greg had sold his dental practice, planning to use it to organize a business of my own. Instead, I used it mostly to research cancer and send emails to family and friends about Greg's and Sherry's health.

After Greg died, Sherry and I sometimes thought up silly questions to ask Google, for fun and to relieve our boredom. When one of the chemo drugs wreaked havoc on Sherry's taste buds, the only food she could taste was green olives. She ate jars of them. What was the difference between the green and black ones? Turns out the answer is ripeness. The unripe green olives and the ripe black ones undergo a curing process, either by being packed in salt, brined, or soaked in oil or water before being eaten. Google had an answer for everything we dreamed up.

Now, I thought a moment about what to enter into the search box, and decided on "advice for widow dating." I got what I expected. An article said there's no time frame about when you should date again; it's different for everyone. That's what the hospice counselor told me about grief. Most of the advice in the article was routine and basic, but one thing leaped out at me. It said that it was common for bereaved spouses to feel like they were cheating when they began dating again. It can take several dates for feelings of guilt to subside, and if they don't go away, then maybe you're not ready yet. I was comforted to know I wasn't alone.

Heart pounding, I did a search for "dating sites." eHarmony was one of the first on the list. I'd seen their advertisements on TV, but had never given them much thought. What harm would there be in doing this for Sherry now? I would just fill in a few blanks and tell her, and that would be that. But when I got onto the website, the questionnaire was long. It reminded me of the Character and Temperament tests that Greg and I gave our employees. The same questions are asked in ten different ways, so your true personality is revealed. Intellectually, I knew there was no need to belabor them. I would just be honest and answer them as quickly as possible. I began. "What is the first thing you would probably notice about me?" Really? The bags under my eyes, my graying hair, and my smile. No matter how intensely sad, lonely, and frightened I felt, I did my best to smile for Sherry.

What was I doing? Had I lost my mind? I shut the computer.

In my robe the next morning, I slipped past Sherry and Chris's bedroom and headed downstairs with my laptop. I put the coffee on. Minutes later, I heard the jingle of the dog's collar. Rose and Olivia ran through the kitchen and family room to the back door. I knew Sherry wouldn't be far behind, because when it came to her dogs, she was an overprotective mother. On occasion, she'd offer to let Olivia sleep with me. I enjoyed those nights with Olivia—her breathing and little heart beating, curled up next to me. I wished it happened more often, but I never asked because I didn't want to take anything away from Sherry.

I took the dogs out. When I came back in, Sherry was sitting at the table in front of my computer.

I pulled my robe tighter around me. A month earlier, when we were out shopping, Sherry had seen it at Nordstorms and sent Chris back to buy it for my birthday. I loved its softness and the sage green color.

I cleared my throat. "Well, I started filling out a profile."

"You did?" She looked up with a big grin. "Awesome. Let me see."

Reaching over her shoulders, I logged in. "It's so hard. How do I answer these questions? Like this one," I said pointing, "What's the first thing you'd probably notice about me?"

"Well, that's easy," Sherry said. "Positive, warm energy."

I appreciated her reminding me how I used to be. I had always worked hard on staying positive, seeing the brighter side of things, no matter how bleak and dismal. But since Greg died, I wasn't sure how I was anymore, because for so many years he had been my gauge. For instance, every time he was grumpy or uptight, it was a signal for me to take note of how I was reacting to the same situation. I prided myself in being the opposite.

I thanked Sherry, sat down and typed in her words. *Positive, warm energy.* It went on like this for at least an hour. I asked the question; she answered. She knew me so well. Three of my best life skills? *Creating a peaceful, beautiful home environment. Resolving conflict. Managing finances.* What was the last book I read and enjoyed? Oh, I could answer that one without her help. *The Glass Castle* by Jeanette Walls. How did my friends describe me? *Affectionate. Caring. Perceptive.*

Optimistic.

When we got towards the end, we needed to upload a photo. We searched through my computer files. There I was dancing with Greg at Sherry's wedding nine years earlier. In another, I stood with Greg and his family while we were in Palm Springs celebrating his parent's 60th wedding anniversary. In this one, I was on the back patio with Greg a few weeks before he died; he was leaning on me instead of his cane. I had no photos of me alone.

"Go take a shower, do your hair and make-up, and I'll take one," Sherry said.

Relieved and excited from all we had accomplished, I went upstairs to fix myself up.

When I returned wearing a new black blouse and blue jeans, Sherry smiled. "Mom, you look gorgeous."

I picked up a piece of mail on the kitchen counter and fanned myself. "I'm a nervous wreck." The reality was sinking in. I'd already jumped off the cliff, and my descent was picking up momentum to a place of no return. "I can't believe we're doing this."

This wasn't the way it was supposed to be.

Sherry wasn't supposed to die before me. I wasn't supposed to be a widow. And now a dating site—an unnatural way to meet someone.

"Over there," Sherry directed me, pointing to the Queen Anne chair in front of a tall ficus.

As I walked past the piano, I mumbled, "this is crazy."

"Come on, Mom," Sherry giggled, "this is fun."

Sitting on the edge of the seat, I asked, "My glasses on or off?"

"Both. Then we'll decide."

I placed my hands in my lap and smiled. When Sherry showed me the photos, I had to admit I didn't look bad for 55. My hair was longer than I'd worn it for years, and the blonde highlights hid the gray. It was possible for someone to see me and not know I was aching inside.

We uploaded one of the pictures, but one last question on the profile remained unanswered: *Some additional information Rhonda wanted you to know is _____.*

I sat quietly. Sherry was still, too. A profound calm came over me, a peace I'd felt only a few times in my life, usually at a low point. It had happened when I gave up trying to solve the problems in my marriage and told Greg I was leaving. As soon as my angry words had slipped out, my body filled with an overwhelming sense of tranquility, assuring me all would be well. Sitting there next to Sherry, in such peace, I thought maybe it was possible some man out there was a match for me, and that he could meet Sherry before she dies. If he met her, he'd understand my great loss...my life, my family. I felt a glimmer of hope. And without further hesitation I typed these words:

"My daughter has terminal cancer, and she's my life right now. Why would I be on a dating site? She's encouraging me to move on with my life. What a treat it would be if you had the opportunity to meet her. She is an angel."

I read the words back to Sherry.

"Perfect, Mom, perfect."

Without another moment's hesitation, I hit the SUBMIT button. There I was, gone forever, my positive, warm energy floating through cyberspace. Sherry and I high-fived and smiled.

Then we began waiting.

Chapter Two

Beginnings

WHEN GREG AND I met in the fall of 1983, it was a new beginning for me. I had recently moved to San Diego and just landed an entry-level position as a receptionist in a dental clinic. On my first day, a co-worker whispered a warning in my ear: "The dentists are arrogant. They don't intermingle with the rest of us. They even have their own lounge to eat in."

The following Monday, while I was eating lunch in the employee breakroom, Greg walked in wearing a white lab-coat, carrying a brown bag. He sat right beside me and smiled. "Hi, I'm Dr. Hayes."

I smiled. "Uh…Hi, I'm Rhonda."

He was so friendly. None of the other doctors had even said good morning.

Greg pulled a sandwich out of the bag. "How long have you been here?" he asked.

The flush from my chest quickly rose to my cheeks. "This is my second week.... I just moved here from Tucson."

With a pug nose, warm smile, and slightly balding head, Greg was more cute than handsome. I felt a physical attraction to him, but I was most impressed by his unassuming nature and the fact that he chose to eat in the employee breakroom rather than the doctors' lounge.

Before he took the first bite of his sandwich, he said, "I only work here on Mondays to supplement my income for my private practice in North County. I'm actually looking for some front office help. Where do you live?"

"Not far, ten minutes." I thought maybe he was offering me a job. I was excited. I knew I wasn't going to survive on the money that the clinic was paying me, but I took the position because my future was sure to be brighter. I didn't want to work as a grocery checker during the day and as a waitress at night like I did when I lived in Tucson. I wanted a chance to have a career and not just a job to pay the bills. I wanted to create a better life for my daughters and myself.

Greg sighed. "Oh…too far. It's a good forty-five minute commute to my office."

I would have been happy to drive further for better pay. But I didn't say anything because I already felt like I was in over my head. There was a lot more to learn about dentistry than I thought there would be. I certainly didn't want to oversell myself to him like I had when I applied for this job at the clinic, but I was desperate to find something. Thank goodness my job was very basic. With no education, all I had was a friendly smile, trim body and blonde hair. All I had to do was make sure patients signed in, collect their co-pay, and tell them to take a seat.

"Too bad," I said, smiling and stirring my yogurt.

"Married? Kids?" he asked.

I was always willing to talk about what was going on in my life, especially if anyone cared to ask. I tucked my shoulder-length hair behind my ear. "I've been divorced for a year and a half. I have two beautiful daughters." Then I continued on with my usual spiel, explaining and apologizing about why I had married so young, at sixteen. I had really wanted to finish high school, go to college and make a decent wage. Instead, I became pregnant.

What I didn't tell him was how I felt the day I learned I was pregnant, when an instantaneous bond formed with that little peanut. When the nurse at Planned Parenthood alluded to the fact that the pregnancy could be terminated, I was offended. I already felt more love than I had ever felt for anyone. My eighteen-year-old boyfriend, Bob, wanted to get married and promised never to raise a hand to me. So like a gale force wind, my life shifted, which was a blessing, because things weren't going so well at home. My mother was on her third abusive husband and had recently given birth to her seventh child. The best she could do was hand me ten dollars and drive me to the Justice of Peace.

By the time I was nineteen, soon after the birth of my second child, I decided that no matter how much I adored my babies, I shouldn't have any more. I feared ending up like my mother. Bob had begun hanging out at the bowling alley and local bars.

Greg stopped eating and leaned towards me.

This encouraged me to keep on talking. I was like a pressure cooker on high heat. I explained how my daughters, eleven-year-old Charlotte and nine-year-old Sherry, and I had moved to San Diego with a man I didn't know all that well. I had doubts it would work out between us, and within weeks, I was certain. So, out of desperation, I sent my girls back to Tucson to stay with Bob and his new girlfriend until I could get myself settled. Charlotte and Sherry had only been gone a few weeks. I was at loose ends without them.

"How about you?" I asked. "Married? Kids?"

Greg shared about his terrible divorce. He told me how angry he was that his ex-wife had moved their children all the way to Sacramento without even telling him. I watched the way his eyes lit up when he described his daughter and son. He told me when he took them hiking, how eight-year-old Kimberly loved studying the acorns, and how Michael, only six, carried a stick and complained about the effort it took to navigate the terrain. Michael loved the beach and the water, while Kimberly wrapped herself in a towel shivering from the cold. I enjoyed listening to him speak about his children. I was pleased to see how much we had in common and thought we could become friends. But when he was finished with lunch, he stood up and said, "It was great to meet you, Rhonda. Got to get back to work."

I don't recall seeing Greg after that. I only worked there for two months before I found a better-paying job with a periodontist.

I rented a room and continued to learn everything I could about dentistry. But with each month my girls were away, I began to worry that someone would think I was an unfit mother.

When I was a young girl, my mother would leave my three older sisters and me, for months at a time, with families we didn't know. We never knew where she went or when she would return. We never heard a word from her. It was confusing and sad. The day my divorce was finalized, my mother explained everything. By then she was divorced, again, living in a trailer park about a half hour away, raising my two younger half-sisters and half-brother. We met for lunch and had a glass of wine. She told me during those times of absence she had given birth to two more babies, fathered by different men. She said giving those babies up for adoption was the most painful thing she ever lived through. I couldn't imagine how hard it would have been to give up Charlotte or Sherry.

Now, even though I wasn't giving up my daughters, the pain of not having them with me was unbearable. At night I would lie awake and wonder if it had been like this for my mother. Of course, I had carefully explained to Charlotte and Sherry why I had to send them back to Tucson, and they seemed to understand. But what if they didn't and were as sad and confused as I was when I was a child? Three or four times a week, I'd write a letter assuring them that as soon as I could, I'd bring them back to live with me. I plastered the envelopes with stickers. They wrote back about how much they loved and missed me, too. I carried those letters around in my purse, rereading them constantly. And even though we talked on the weekends, it wasn't enough. I missed the daily chatter, fighting, and giggling. I missed the smell of their shampooed hair and their kisses.

In April 1984, just before my 30th birthday, I attended the Anaheim Dental Convention with some of my co-workers. I'd never been to anything like it before. I walked past each booth looking at the dental instruments and impression materials. Then, in the mass of strangers, I heard a voice call out.

"Rhonda, it's so good to see you."

I looked up and recognized his face, but I couldn't remember his name.

"Doctor...uh." I blushed with embarrassment.

"Dr. Hayes...Greg."

"Oh yeah," I said, and smiled. "Are you still at the clinic?"

"Yes, but hopefully not much longer," he said, smiling back.

I relaxed, recalling our conversation six months earlier in the employee breakroom.

"How are your kids?" I asked.

"I'll have them for a month this summer," he said. "What about yours?"

The answer was complicated. Things had not gone well with Bob and his girlfriend, so the girls had gone to stay with Bob's parents. I had a good relationship with my ex-in-laws and we agreed it would be best if the girls stayed until the end of the school year.

"Mine are coming next month." I smiled. "For good."

Greg gently touched my shoulder and said, "I missed your smiling face. Obviously, you're working somewhere else. Where?"

"For Dr. Silverstein in La Mesa," I said. I was proud to be working for a specialist. It was a nice office, much better than the clinic.

"The periodontist? I know who he is." Greg paused, then raised his eyebrows like he had just come up with an idea. "Hey, want to come to the UCLA Alumni party? It's at five o'clock...a lot of fun. Drinks, food."

I thought this would be the perfect opportunity to get to know him better, but several of us had carpooled, and I didn't know what time we were leaving. "Thanks, I'll try," I said.

I didn't make it to the party and figured I'd blown it with Greg, but the following week he called me at work. "I missed you at the party," he said. I was thrilled to hear his voice. This guy really was paying attention to me. First he remembered my name and now where I worked.

"I'm so sorry," I said. Realizing now that he really cared, I wished that I had made more of an effort. "Everyone wanted to leave early to beat the traffic."

"Well, will you go out to dinner with me on Saturday night?"

"I can't," I said, and sighed. "I'm doing some volunteer work in exchange for free summer day camp for my girls." This poor guy. I didn't want him to give up. I really was interested. It would be the perfect time to get to know him better, before Charlotte and Sherry came back and I still had some free time.

"Please call and ask me again," I said.

"Well how about the following weekend?" he asked. That was the weekend I was driving over to pick Charlotte and Sherry up. The weekend I'd been dreaming of since they had left months ago.

"I'm going to Tucson to pick up my girls," I said, "but I'd really love to have dinner with you."

We arranged for a date the Saturday night after that.

My reunion with Charlotte and Sherry was joyful, with lots of hugging and laughing. How much taller they'd grown in just six months. Charlotte and I stood back to back while

Sherry judged to see who was taller. Charlotte had learned the latest music and bands. She was spraying her bangs up like Madonna and hiding her new body under bulky tee-shirts. Sherry had learned how to cross-stitch and crochet. Her legs were long and lanky, her teeth big and jumbled. Her sandy-blonde hair was short now, cut evenly from the crown of her head all the way around in a bowl cut. They said their good-byes to their grandparents while I loaded their clothes and stuffed animals into the trunk of my Chevy.

After arriving in San Diego, the three of us shared a long, narrow bedroom. The girls slept on twin mattresses, shoved end to end, up against the wall. From my full-size bed, I looked at them as they talked about the friends they were meeting at day camp.

They begged me to repeat the story about when I was a young girl, fantasizing about my grownup life. *I'm standing in a spotless kitchen. It's painted bright yellow. I wave good-bye to my husband as he leaves for work. I never see his face. We never kiss. All I'm able to see about him is that he wears a tie.* That's it. To me, it represented everything that I hoped for in life...love, safety, and security. The three things I had needed as a child and thought I would have when I married Bob. The three of us laughed. And then I reminded them again, "Don't do as I did. Get your education first before you get married and have babies."

But thoughts of Greg were not far from my mind. How was I going to tell Charlotte and Sherry about my upcoming date? For months, I had been promising them that when we were reunited it would be just the three of us—but I had a strong feeling that things were going to work out between Greg and me. So before I told them about Greg, I made a big deal about how we would never be separated again.

Then, one night when the moment felt right, I said, "I met a nice man."

"Yeah!" said Sherry.

I glanced over at Charlotte. I could tell by the look in her eye that she wasn't thrilled. "Where did you meet him?" she asked.

I smiled. "When I was working at the clinic. He's asked me out for Saturday night." Then I quickly changed the subject. "Do you guys want mac-n-cheese for dinner that night?"

They said yes.

On Saturday night when the doorbell rang at our small apartment, Sherry raced to the door and squinted through the peephole. "Mom, he's wearing a tie!" she yelled. My pulse quickened. I was happy to see Sherry's surprise and now Charlotte's excitement. I felt it, too. No date had ever showed up wearing a tie before, but there Greg stood in a collared shirt, khaki pants, and a blue striped tie.

Thirty minutes into our date, while Greg and I were standing in line to see the movie *Behold Hawaii*, he took my hand and said, "Do you want to go to real Hawaii with me?" I could hardly believe my ears. I didn't know if he was serious, but I didn't want to discourage him in any way, so I smiled and said, "Sure."

After the movie, we went to dinner. The restaurant overlooked the bay and downtown San Diego. We settled into our booth and talked endlessly about our children and ourselves, completely unaware of everything going on around us.

I talked about my childhood, my father. The only memory I have of my biological father is of him holding a gun to my mother's head. One of my stepfathers molested me. Another beat my mother. Greg reached across the table and held my hand. I also told him how disappointing it was to find out that Bob wasn't the kind of father I hoped he would be. I thought he would grow flowers in the backyard instead of marijuana. I thought he'd read the girls stories at bedtime, but instead he taught them the lyrics of Pink Floyd's "We Don't Need No Education." I told him how guilty I felt when Sherry needed help with her schoolwork, but I was too busy working and too tired to help. By the time she reached third grade, she struggled even more, so she ended up repeating it. I was so grateful that she never complained about being held back.

Greg talked about how idyllic his childhood and college days were, and what a nightmare his divorce had been. He poured the last bit of wine and gazed into my eyes. At some point, we managed to come back to reality, looking up to find no one left in the dining room. We laughed, noticing our waiter standing off in a distant corner, politely waiting for us to pay the tab and leave.

That was our last date alone that summer. The next afternoon Greg came back after he'd gone to church with his parents. He took the girls and me to the beach. All afternoon he tirelessly showed and instructed us how to bodysurf. He seemed like a natural father, the kind I'd longed for. I appreciated that he wasn't paying attention only to me, like the other man I'd dated. I could already see my ideal family forming.

We had a wonderful few months, as Charlotte and Sherry settled into their new life in San Diego and we all settled into a life that included Greg. When Greg's kids arrived for their summer visit, our "dates" became more chaotic, with twice as many kids as adults. But the six of us managed to squeeze into Greg's car without too much complaining. We went to Padres games, Balboa Park, and Oceanside Harbor.

At the end of the summer, when Greg's children left to go back home, I was surprised and deeply touched when he cried after they boarded the plane. I never imagined that a father could miss his children so much.

That night, Greg put his arm around my shoulder and said, "At least I have you and your girls. Do you want to move in?"

He knew my lease was coming up and that I had been looking for another place. Greg's two-bedroom, two-bath condo was nestled in a grove of Eucalyptus trees. It was small, but its unique layout made it more than adequate for all of us.

He wanted the whole package of we three, and I felt I had good reason to trust him. I loved everything about him. So I said yes.

Three months after we moved in, Greg kept his promise and booked a trip to Maui. He made arrangements for his dental assistant to come stay with the girls for the week. As soon as we boarded the plane, I got my first taste of Hawaii. Each flight attendant wore a red, white, and blue Muumuu with a hibiscus clipped in her hair. Romantic Hawaiian music filled the cabin. I wondered if Greg was planning to propose. Our week was filled with body surfing, snorkeling, hiking, parasailing, and driving the winding road to Hana. At sunset, we watched the sand blush with all shades of pink. We ate mangos, papayas, and pineapple. We made love. We had a fun and romantic week, but what really stood out was the morning we played tennis.

On our first date, when Greg asked if I played, I said, "Yes," remembering back to the times when a girlfriend and I went out and batted around a few balls. So when he suggested it, I quickly agreed. Full of enthusiasm, we stopped at the front desk to get rackets and balls. Out on the court, Greg popped open the can of balls and served. I swung and missed. He served slower. I missed, again and again. This went on for a short while, then he told me to wait and came back with a bucket of balls. This time he stood at the net, throwing each ball directly to the face of my racket. We built up a rhythm. Finally able to connect with the ball, I was excited. I ran to the net and thanked him. He kissed me and said, "No problem. I'm investing in our future."

I appreciated and loved him for taking the time. This was what I longed for as a child. Countless times, I sat at my mother's piano trying to teach myself how to play. In third grade, my music teacher taught me about FACE and Every Good Boy Does Fine, but that's all I ever learned. I would stare at my mother's complicated music, trying to make sense of it. My mother didn't have the money to pay for lessons, but it wouldn't have cost anything for her to teach me. I wanted to fill our house up with music because she couldn't. She was too busy working, getting divorced, or having another baby. By the time I reached eleven, still sitting at the bench, frustrated and a bit resentful, I finally gave up.

When we returned home from Maui, Greg and I continued rallying on the tennis courts. I began to see another side to him, a competitive edge. In school, I took PE, but never any extracurricular competitive sports. At home, I'd constantly do round-offs, back bends, and the splits, but the only competition was with myself. On the tennis court, when Greg put a back-spin on the ball, making me miss, I got very frustrated. I thought he was being mean, and I wanted to quit. But he wouldn't let me, saying he couldn't wait for the day when I was able to pass him at the net. So I kept playing, holding out hope for that day.

He had a different kind of competitive nature when it came to playing games. He taught Sherry how to play backgammon. They'd play until the clock struck nine—her bed time. But when he didn't win the final game, he'd cross his arms like a spoiled child and bark, "You just got lucky." At first, I thought he was joking. But he wasn't. He'd insist on playing past her bedtime, until he won.

At other times he was unreasonable and too strict with the girls. He micromanaged who ate a cookie, who was too noisy getting ready for school, or who didn't acknowledge him when he walked into the room. Sometimes, for punishment, he made them go outside and run up and down stairs near our house. He ran alongside them, badgering them like a drill sergeant.

I felt ashamed of myself as I stood by watching the sweat and tears running down their faces. My heart ached. They were good girls. They didn't deserve this. I wanted to speak up, but I stayed quiet, trying to support Greg, while at the same time fearing I was becoming my mother.

On Saturdays, when I took Charlotte and Sherry shopping or out to lunch, sometimes they'd complain about how harsh Greg could be. I listened to them and nodded. I understood their feelings. Yes, he could be tough and unreasonable, but he loved all three of us.

After living together for a year, Greg asked me to marry him. I was washing the dishes. He was in the living room watching ESPN. During a commercial break, he yelled, "Don't you think it's about time we got married?"

It wasn't the romantic moment I'd envisioned, but I was relieved and happy. Water dripping from my fingertips, I ran over and kissed him. "Yes, I'd love to."

Later that evening when we made the announcement to the girls, the first thing they wanted to know was when they could call him Dad.

Greg smiled. "You can start now."

Chapter Three

Blended Family

IN MARCH OF 1986, we had an intimate ceremony and a festive reception in Greg's parents' backyard. I wore a crown of flowers in my hair and an ivory tea-length skirt and lace blouse. Greg wore a black suit, white shirt, and paisley tie. It was Greg's idea to have all four children take part in the vows, accepting each other as family. It was touching, we were all so happy.

Home from our honeymoon, I went to work for Greg in

his dental practice. We had talked about it for months and had no idea if we could be together day and night, but it made sense to try. We agreed that if either one of us had a problem, I would quit and go to work for another dentist. From the first day on, I loved seeing how kind and gentle Greg was with his patients. We had the same work ethic and values, and treated each other as professionals—no one would suspect we were married. It wasn't that we tried to hide it. We just didn't bring it up, though one time I slipped and called him "Honey" in the hallway. We laughed.

In addition to working, Greg encouraged me to take a few classes at the community college. He knew this is what I had wanted to do since I was fourteen, after my mother married her third husband. One night, after they'd gone out, he beat her up in the car on the way home. It was devastating to see her bloody and bruised. I didn't know what to do. For days she walked around in a trance. I hated him for hurting her. I thought she should leave him, but she didn't. This is when I quit having fantasies and began thinking about college.

Taking Greg's advice, I signed up for remedial English and math. Every night, the girls and I gathered around the dining room table to do our homework while he tutored whoever needed his help. I was struggling. I knew I'd never be able to help Charlotte and Sherry with their algebra and biology, and was impressed when he rattled off explanations about photosynthesis, evolution, and the quadratic equation. He never bragged about his academic awards and accomplishments, and always used simple, understandable language. As the years passed, the girls and I took more difficult classes, and I continued to be amazed by Greg's intelligence. When he lectured Charlotte and Sherry about applying for scholarships and the importance of developing good study habits, I began to realize why I had been so lost in high school. By the time I dropped out to get married, I'd already attended four high schools. I never had time to connect with a teacher or mentor, and barely made a friend to eat lunch with. Grateful for what Greg was doing, not only for me, but for my daughters, I joked about being one of his kids.

But honestly, I wondered why such a smart man would have married me. One night while getting ready for bed, I asked him.

He turned around and said, "You had potential."

Not sure how to respond, I quietly slipped under the covers thinking how much easier it would've been if he had said, "Because I love you."

By now, outside of work, I should've been used to his undermining remarks.

When Charlotte made the cheerleading squad, he congratulated her, but added that cheerleaders were worthless because they didn't understand the game of football.

I'd cower with embarrassment when he shook his finger at a driver because she wasn't driving the way he thought she should be.

At times, I tried to explain to Greg how hurtful he could be, but he would discount and trivialize what I had to say. This would upset me, but I'd let it go, hoping it wouldn't happen again.

After all, he wasn't an unfair man. He demanded a lot from himself. He pushed himself at the gym, on the ski slopes, and the tennis court like his life depended upon it. On the weekends, he built fences, planted trees, flowers, and vegetables. His body twisting and sweating, he weeded the garden, mowed, and edged the lawn. He worked hard for his Rotary Club, taking on board and officer responsibilities.

After Charlotte graduated from high school, she enrolled at the same community college I was still attending part time. We even took some of the same classes, sitting together taking notes, excited to support each other. Greg thought since we were saving on a university tuition for Charlotte that we could afford to pay rent for her to live somewhere else. I agreed with him about the money and that it would be good for Charlotte to be on her own. Within days, Charlotte was ecstatic because she'd found the perfect roommate in a nearby neighborhood. I would miss having her at home, but looked forward to a break from hearing Greg's lectures and sarcastic remarks to her.

During Sherry's senior year, she worked part time in the practice with Greg and me. She filed patients' charts, sterilized instruments, and helped wherever she was needed.

She and I grew even closer. Now that she was experiencing both sides of Greg — work and home — she understood the best and worst of him. While Charlotte moved on with her teaching career and her own relationships, Sherry became my new confidant. Sherry's objective way of thinking about Greg was refreshing.

A year later, when Sherry left home for Cal Poly Pomona, I had mixed feelings. On one hand, a sense of freedom washed over me. Greg and I had pretty much completed our jobs as parents. The girls had turned out to be healthy, happy, well-adjusted young women. On the other hand, I was sad to see Sherry go. I had lost the closeness with Charlotte, and now I was losing my connection with Sherry, too.

Greg and I sold the house in which we'd raised the girls and bought a new one that we considered our sanctuary, a ranch-style home in a rural area, with beautiful views of the mountains. I thought that we would feel like honeymooners, and in many ways we did. We explored our eight-year relationship on a new level. Specifically, we discussed how a husband and wife could fall into the trap of taking on parent-child roles with each other instead of behaving as two adults. With such conversations, we opened Pandora's box.

I wondered if I was attracted to Greg because he was such a strong parent figure, if my feelings of discontent with him were my fault. At thirty-nine, I still wished I had a father, though I knew I should be getting over that. Maybe Greg had been attracted to me because he knew I was a push-over. I'm not sure which one of us closed the box, but we soon stopped having those discussions.

I began meditating more frequently. When I was young, I had learned about meditation from my mother's friends George and Doris. They were an older, childless couple who had taken a special interest in my sisters and me. Doris taught us how to sew, garden, and cook. George taught us how to do headstands, yoga poses, and sit still and chant "Om." Although, as a child, I hadn't understood the principles behind the chanting, I now found myself repeating over and over, "God is with me. I am at peace." I said it while I was sitting in meditation, driving, washing the dishes, and folding the laundry. Looking back now, I suppose that, more than anything else, I wanted to believe I was at peace.

But I wasn't—and things got worse. I was becoming the badgered step-daughter. It seemed no matter what I did, or didn't do, I couldn't please Greg. I didn't fold the laundry, take a photo, hold his hand, or chew my food correctly. I always tried to do everything exactly the way he liked, and when I tried to explain that to him, he acted like he didn't believe me. So I would end up in tears, and he would say I couldn't take a joke.

But I knew he wasn't joking, and that started a slow burn of resentment and anger in me. Instead of dealing with those feelings, though, I pushed them away and told myself things would get better. I tried harder to please him.

One fall evening, I came home from work to find that our house had been burglarized. The TV, stereo, and my jewelry were gone. Every drawer had been gone through, even the ones holding my panties and bras. This violation triggered a wave of emotion. Depressed, I moved as if stuck in wet concrete. A month after the break-in, I needed every ounce of energy to drag myself out of bed and get ready for work. As soon as I got out of the shower, the tears would start. The more I tried to stop them, the harder they flowed. The only thing I was capable of doing was slipping back under the covers.

Greg was worried about me, though he didn't actually say it. Normally, he wouldn't stand for me being "lazy." I was relieved he didn't give me a hard time on the days I crawled back into bed. He kissed me on the forehead and quietly left for the office. I knew I needed help, but I couldn't do it for myself. I didn't have thoughts of suicide. I just wanted to get in my car and drive forever. This went on for three months, until one day Greg gave me the phone number of a psychiatrist he knew. I was tired of being tired, but the only reason I made the call was I thought he would be someone who could help me really sort things out. I had been telling friends, family, and even Greg that my depression was because of the burglary, but I knew there was more to it.

I did my best to explain my feelings to the doctor. I didn't want to feel like Greg's child. I wanted to be his wife. But he sat behind his desk peering over reading glasses, babbling on about medications and how they interacted with each other. I didn't want two different prescriptions. I wanted to be *heard*. But, in order to be heard, I would first need to learn how to speak. Instead, now, I lowered my head, defeated, and left with the prescriptions.

Greg and the psychiatrist were right: the anti-depressants did make me feel better. I was able to function, get back to work, and even enrolled in my last two classes for my associates degree. Receiving my diploma inspired me.

A few months later, while we were eating dinner, I said, "I'd really like to go on and get my bachelor's."

Greg furrowed his brow. "Well, what do you want to be?"

I sighed, "Oh, I don't know." I immediately regretted being so lackadaisical. He wouldn't be happy with my vague answer. I was frustrated that I had no clear career vision. Something was off kilter, but I couldn't put my finger on it. In part, I didn't want to be left behind. Greg was the dentist, Charlotte the teacher, and Sherry the dental hygienist. Everyone in my family had a role, an identity. What was I going to be, an office worker in my husband's practice?

Greg sat back in his chair and threaded his fingers, "Well, I can't support it unless you have something very specific that you want to do."

I took a sip of wine and conjured up a vision of myself sitting behind a desk wearing a business suit. I thought how nice it would be to feel respected. My face reddened as I blurted out, "I want to be in business...to work for IBM."

Greg rolled his eyes. "I want to travel, and if you're

working for someone else you know you can't take off anytime you want." He cleared his throat. "You know I depend upon you."

I knew he depended on me to keep his practice running smoothly, but I wanted to hear him say how much he appreciated me. Instead, I felt defeated. But I couldn't express what I needed. I couldn't even come up with a specific career I wanted to pursue.

I poured a little more wine. "Yeah, I suppose you're right. I suppose it's not a great idea."

I never learned how to ask. I either wished or thought that Greg would eventually get it through osmosis. The following summer, Greg and I were hiking in Ireland. The view was like a scene out of a movie. Free roaming sheep peppered the steep grassy hillsides. When we reached the hill's crest, we sat to rest and I took his hand. "Greg, I need to talk."

He jerked his hand away. "What?"

"You've been so cold. What's going on?"

"Nothing, goddamn it. You're in Ireland."

It wasn't my idea to go. His parents wanted their three children and spouses to go with them to celebrate their 50th wedding anniversary.

"I need you…. I need to feel loved. I'm hurting." I pulled my shoulders back, feeling confident that I'd succeeded in being specific.

He stood up. "I fucking love you!" he shouted.

I felt my adrenalin pump. "Okay—then adore me, appreciate me!"

He shot me a look of disgust. "Yes! Dear! Got! It!"

I could hardly choke out the word. "Good," I said, but what I thought to myself was...*You jerk!*

A year later, Charlotte and Sherry announced their engagements on the same weekend. It surprised them as much as it did Greg and me. We were all thrilled. For months, I stayed busy with bridal showers and dress shopping. They were living their lives as I'd hoped they would, first college then career. Then they'd marry for love and have children.

The week after I turned forty-six, I was mother of the bride. Sherry was first, with a large formal church wedding. She was a beautiful bride, her face radiating under the veil. Greg wore a black tuxedo, holding his chin high as he escorted her down the aisle. Chris anxiously waited at the altar. He was ten years older than Sherry, but no one would've guessed it—the dimples in his cheeks deepened with his big smile. That day, they were Cinderella and Prince Charming, which was also the theme of their reception.

Four months later, Charlotte and Stuart opted for a small elegant beachside wedding in La Jolla. Charlotte's long blonde hair swept against her tanned shoulders and strapless A-line wedding gown. Stuart wearing a black tux with a white bow-tie, grinned from ear to ear. As they exchanged their vows, the waves rolled in and the sun set. Tears of happiness trickled down my cheeks.

My daughters had their education, careers, and now wonderful husbands.

That fall, Greg and I traveled to Belgium, Switzerland, Italy, and France with his parents. We all got along so well. I was glad he'd warned me that if I had gone on to get my bachelor's degree and worked at IBM, we wouldn't have been able to take such trips.

A year later, Sherry came back to work in the office as our dental hygienist. Greg, Sherry, and I had lunch together, reminiscing about the old days when she filed charts and cleaned the office, and I smiled when they launched into clinical conversations about dentistry. The rest of the office staff was reliable and worked well together, too. Charlotte was teaching middle school and working on her master's. Things were going so well I thought I should go off the anti-depressants, but every time I brought it up, Greg refused to hear of it, reminding me how horrible I had felt after the burglary.

In January 2003, after returning from Greg's lifetime dream trip of traveling through New Zealand, he noticed he had some swelling in one testicle. During our trip, we'd ridden Harley-Davidsons 1,500 miles on the South Island, so thought the swelling was from that. But it wasn't. It was a rare, fast-growing Non-Hodgkin's Lymphoma. Catching it early, the doctors put him on a chemotherapy regimen that seemed manageable for a strong, healthy fifty-three-year-old.

Halfway through Greg's chemo, I woke one night to go to the bathroom. When I came back to bed, I touched his chest. It felt like fire. Panicking, I called his name, shaking him awake.

He opened his eyes and whispered, "Honey, this is serious…must be an infection. I might not make it."

The possibility of him not making it had never crossed my mind. I couldn't imagine life without him. No matter how many times he frustrated and hurt me, I loved him.

Fortunately, within weeks the antibiotics had cleared up the infection. Six months' later, his eyelashes, eyebrows, and most of his hair had grown back. His follow-up tests showed no signs of cancer. He was again riding his Harley, working out, and golfing. Everything was back to normal.

But what if he hadn't survived? What would I do with the practice? Without Greg, the practice couldn't exist. I wouldn't have a job. We didn't have any life insurance. What would I do with the house and the acre of land? I couldn't take care of it by myself.

Feeling vulnerable about all the things I'd have to face, I began thinking of solutions.

Understanding the benefits of being self-employed, I ultimately thought of starting up my own business. Excited, I knew I could help small businesses set up bookkeeping/organizing systems.

I studied and became QuickBooks Certified. I came up with a catchy name for my business: Help Me, Rhonda. After getting my license, I joined an organizing group and secured a few clients. Greg seemed happy and supportive, as long as it didn't interfere with my full-time work at his office.

One evening, I broached the subject. "What do you think about me working less hours in the office and more on my business?"

"If you're quitting, then so am I!"

"Well—if that's what you want, that would be okay," I said. I would have to work hard to build up my clientele to pay for everything, but that didn't concern me. I was a hard worker, and we had savings. Greg and I had always lived within our means and recently paid off the mortgage. Maybe I could make enough on my own to handle all the bills. I said, "Let's do it."

I thought he would agree—but he didn't. Instead, he said he wanted to sell the house and the practice and move to Green Valley, Arizona, a retirement community south of Tucson.

I was shocked.

About six months earlier, we had driven to Green Valley for a weekend because Greg wanted to check out the area that some of his golfing buddies had told him about. He had really gotten into golf by then and had given up his Harley. While looking at the model homes, Greg said we'd be better off to buy a house right then while they were so cheap. When I hesitated, he said if we decided to retire and move there it would be at least five years down the road. Five years was a long way off. By then, I'd probably be ready. So in the matter of two hours that Sunday afternoon, we picked out cabinets, counter-tops, and flooring for a tract house that still needed to be built.

Little did I know that Greg's real intentions were to move as soon as the house was completed.

When he finally told me, I didn't know how to say no. So like always, I gave in. I started packing, consoling myself that my sister Joline was still in Tucson, and Charlotte and Stuart had recently moved to Phoenix for her PhD program at ASU.

I had just turned fifty-one and Greg was fifty-six when we left Southern California to go live the retirement life in Green Valley. My world had been jerked out from under me.

The practice I helped build, our home with the view of the mountains, and my business all vanished.

Chapter Four

Awakening

I'D ALWAYS HEARD GREAT stories about retirement parties and roasts. I knew people received elaborate gold watches, framed letters, and engraved plaques for their years of service. Even as a child, I was in awe when my mother showed me her father's retirement pin—DuPont engraved on the tiny pin with a diamond embedded under its name. When my mother died, it was the one thing I wanted. It's still in my jewelry box.

One night, soon after arriving in Green Valley, Greg and I were sitting in the courtyard drinking a vodka tonic, and he was talking about the good retirement life. But I felt slighted. If my working life was over, I wanted some kind of closure or commendation, like his warmly worded letters of recommendation for our employees. I tried to explain my feelings to him. For me, it didn't need to be anything special, a simple "thank you" would be enough.

Greg sat there rolling his eyes. "Your retirement is your thank you."

I rubbed my shoulders. "But can you just say thank you?"

He couldn't.

So, I stayed busy, meeting new friends, working out, golfing, swimming, volunteering, and taking piano lessons.

But I still wasn't happy. Everything felt wrong.

Greg and I had stupid arguments about the laundry, decorating, and how I parked my car. No matter what happened, it was either something I did, or didn't do, that made him irritable. I kept track, by writing in a journal, so I could prove to myself that I wasn't going crazy.

One night at a party, while waiting in line for the bathroom, I asked the older women behind me how retirement was going for her. Her soft face contorted, as if she'd read my mind. She said, "Honey, they all become experts at what we've been doing for years. They need power, control."

I decided I needed to go back to work. Angry at Greg, I wanted nothing to do with dentistry and applied to be a customer service representative for an accountant software company. With my QuickBooks experience, I was hired right away, but the job was to help solve technical difficulties, which I knew very little about. I worked 60 hours a week. It was stressful and paid very little. I was exhausted and relieved when the tax season was over.

I had proved to myself that I was capable of getting work on my own, but I still wasn't happy.

One September night, while writing in my journal, I questioned if I might be falling out of love with Greg. Overwhelmed by the possibility, my tears dropped onto the page. Then I wrote words I'd never written before: *Dear God, please help me.*

Little did I realize that help was on the way.

The following week, I drove up to Phoenix to visit Charlotte and Stuart.

Before I left, Greg followed me down the hallway, toward the garage, and said, "I want you to call me while you're up there."

"Okay," I said, hoisting my suitcase into the trunk.

"Did you hear me?" He shook his finger in my face. "Last time, I had to call you first."

When did I last go anywhere without him? And who called who first?

Two hours later, I pulled into Charlotte's driveway and called Greg.

"Hi," I said, "I'm calling to let you know that I'm here."

"Well, good. Thanks for calling," he said, and hung up.

The last night of my visit, Charlotte handed me *The Verbally Abusive Relationship,* by Patricia Evans.

"Mom," she said, "you might want to read this."

Verbal abuse?

Charlotte explained how her friend Julie had suggested she read it when she was struggling with an ex-boyfriend in college. "This book taught me what covert verbal abuse means. It was life changing for me."

Before I began to read, I called Greg. I looked at the clock: 9:35.

Four rings. Strange. Why didn't he answer? He always stayed up later than me.

I left a message. "I'm calling to tell you good night. I love you."

As I settled into bed and began to read, everything became clear. Initially, the word *abuse* sounded so harsh. I never imagined that Greg was abusive, because there was no hitting, name-calling, or cheating. If that were the case, I would have known what to do. As I read, I learned more about the patterns indicating verbal abuse. How manipulating, controlling, and undermining can be as subtle as a dripping faucet, yet eventually succeeds in eroding a partner's self-esteem. Evans calls it crazy-making, because you're constantly questioning and doubting yourself. At times, Greg was a down-right jerk, but mostly he was covert and unpredictable. I would think everything was great, then all of a sudden he would blow up, say something hurtful, or give me a look of disgust. I read all night, feeling a mixture of pain and relief.

In the morning, I called Greg again. He didn't answer, so I left another message. "Hi, sweetie, it's me. I assume you're golfing, but I'm concerned."

Ten minutes later, he called back.

"I got your message last night. But I didn't answer because I was so pissed at you I couldn't see straight. How dare you call after nine! You know the curfew."

Curfew? What the hell was he talking about? I would never win with this man. I whispered, "I'm sorry," and hung up.

I walked out to the kitchen where Charlotte was preparing breakfast. I choked on my tears. "I just talked to your dad."

After hearing the story, she said, "Mom, he's wrong!" She clenched her fist. "The wife calls any time she wants. That curfew was for Sherry and me when we were teenagers."

When I arrived home, Greg was still out golfing. I waited in the den with the book in my hand. The garage door opened and closed, then the soles of Greg's shoes hit the tiled floor. When he paused at the den's doorway, I shook the book in the air and said, "I'm leaving you." In my next breath, a heavenly peace washed over me. I didn't intend to say those words, and had never said them before.

Greg sat down next to me. "Let's talk," he said. "Where

are you going?"

Going? I hadn't planned on going anywhere.

"Please don't tell me you're leaving unless you mean it," Greg said. "You're right…, I do verbally abuse you, because you let me."

I looked up and saw his tears. I asked, holding it up so he could see the cover, "Have you read this book?"

"No, but I know what I do." He took my hand, "I love you. I can't stand the thought of you leaving. Will you help me?"

The next two days, we talked and cried. I began to feel hopeful. The morning of the third day, I began writing a letter to our families. It was important to ask for their help. When I showed it to Greg, he began revising it, finally saying, "This is good. I like it." We agreed to send it to our children and our siblings—the ones who we believed were most impacted.

"We'll get through this—I promise," I said. "I'm mailing them in the morning."

"Okay."

The next morning, after Greg left to go golfing, I dropped copies of the letter for each family member in the community mailbox.

Dear Family,

This is a first for me, but I am going to ask all of you for your help in a very specific way. As most of you know, I have been dealing with depression and a general feeling of confusion about my life for a long time. In the past year and a half, I have been suffering more than ever. I have already shared that fact with some of you and want to let you know exactly what is happening. Through counseling, talking, journaling, praying, and most recently by reading the book The Verbally Abusive Relationship *by Patricia Evans, I have clarified the core of my pain and struggle.*

Please understand that I love Greg very much. This is not *a personal attack on Greg in any way; this is about helping him. This is* not *about me trying to look like a victim; this is about helping me to recover and rebuild my spirit and soul. I have never learned to protect my boundaries and have gotten very good at "stuffing" my pain.*

The reason I am writing this letter is because I know that some of you have personally been a part of this abuse. It has been more painful for me to see my loved ones be subjected to this unacceptable behavior than to be subjected to it myself. If you have felt in any way that you have been a part of this, I highly recommend you read the book and you will understand why we need your help. I realize that I can no longer hold that sense of responsibility to "fix it" for all of you, which I could never do anyway, but always tried. It is going to take every bit of my energy right now to do what I need to do for me.

I reached my breaking point recently and felt that there was no more that I could do to save my spirit or my marriage. Greg and I had a very serious talk and he has admitted to being abusive to me and others. Please understand that he does not want to "hurt" anyone. He has just gotten very good at getting what he wants in very covert and overt ways that make you question yourself. He takes full responsibility for his actions. There are very specific techniques to use that will help end the abuse. It is very much like training a dog with a firm, immediate response for the unacceptable action. Again, that is why I recommend that you read the book if you feel that you have been abused in any way. I am practicing these techniques and I will do it! Greg agrees that he will stop the abuse only if I/we stop him immediately as it is happening. He has agreed to go to marriage counseling with me if we cannot resolve this issue. He has agreed that I have every right to leave him if I do my part and he does not change. There is no question in my mind or heart that he is committed to this change. Greg has read this letter and fully agrees that I can put it in the mail to all of you.

I have never felt this empowered in my life. I want you to know how much I love all of you and I appreciate all of your love and support. This is a personal celebration and I am totally free to love myself by setting my own boundaries without guilt or concern and still be with the man whom I love so deeply. This is also a personal celebration for Greg because he does not intentionally want to abuse; but has said things in unkind ways to us all and now he wants to change. Please know that this is a very positive thing for all of us. Love, Rhonda and Greg

When Greg returned from golf, he barked, "Did you mail them?" Before I could respond to his question he continued, "Our family has nothing to do with this."

My heart pounded. What's he talking about? Family has nothing to do with this? He treated Charlotte and Sherry, grown married women, like they were still living under our roof. What the hell is talking about? The family has nothing to do with this? They have as much to do with this as I do.

He continued. "This is between us—besides, we hardly see family anymore."

I set my jaw. I had to hold my ground. "Greg, they'll understand. We need support."

"Rhonda, I'm telling you, it was wrong!" he yelled. "You shouldn't have done it!"

"Well, it's done. I can't get them back. You agreed."

He slammed his fist on the table. "Oh, does that mean I'm verbally abusing you?"

"Don't make me second-guess myself…. STOP!" I screamed.

His eyebrows rose. He pointed his index finger upward as if he just come up with a great idea. "Hey, I've got it. Tomorrow's Sunday. I'll call everyone and tell them they're getting a letter, but if they respect us, they should tear it up without reading it."

"No! It's not a mistake!" I shouted. "Why are you so afraid of the truth?"

The next morning, it was difficult to crawl out of bed, but

at least the letters were in the mail. He couldn't change that. We avoided each other. I buried my head in the newspaper, while he paced outside talking on his cell phone. I wondered who he was talking to.

Later that afternoon, Greg said, "Well, I can tell you one thing, no one is happy with you."

"Really? Why?" I asked.

"I told them about the letter." He folded his arms across his chest. "You're going to regret this."

"What did you tell them?" I asked, placing my hands on my hips.

He shook his finger at me. "That a shocking letter is coming from you!"

My heart pounded. "Greg we agreed to send that letter! Who did you call?"

"It doesn't matter. Everyone's pissed at you!"

The thought of everyone being mad at me was crushing. I wondered what he said to my siblings and all our children that could make them angry with me.

"Hey, I've got another idea," he said, "Send an email and tell them to tear it up without reading it."

I lowered my head, defeated again. "Well, maybe."

"Yeah, that's it. Come on, honey."

Later that night, I sat down at the computer while Greg sat across the room staring me down, calling out orders. "Don't read it! Tear it up."

I began to type:

I know that you've spoken with Greg and you're aware of

the letter in the mail to you. I felt that it was a positive, proactive approach for helping us solve our issues. Now, I think I mailed it out of desperation. I needed all the support I could get. Now I'm questioning myself whether or not you need to be involved at all.

My fingers stopped. My heart pounded to the rhythm of the blinking cursor.

Greg continued. "Tear it up! We made a mistake."

A calm came over me. There was no doubt in my mind that God was there helping me. I continued to type words that I knew Greg wouldn't approve:

If you would like to read it, go ahead. Please understand my frame of mind. I love you all very much and want you to know that we will survive this and somewhere down the road we can all laugh about it. Love, Rhonda

I hit Send.

All I heard was the tapping of his fingers on the chair's arm.

I looked him straight in the eye. "Where's your faith? You have to quit running."

His shoulders relaxed as if he had hit bottom and laid the shovel down. A spiritual awakening. It's impossible to say exactly how Greg felt at that very moment, but for myself, I felt pure love, similar to the bond with Charlotte when I was just pregnant at sixteen. Only this time there was no baby. I was the one who was receiving all the love.

Two days later, while looking for some Advil, I found a

yellow Post-it stuck on the inside of the door of Greg's medicine cabinet. It said: Be kind to Rhonda. Tell her more often that I love her. I stood there for a moment and held it close to my chest, then put it back. As I walked out into the hallway, I caught a glimpse of Greg in the living room. He was sitting with his palms open, resting on his knees. I had seen him meditate before a church service, but never at home.

I, too, had to remind myself every day to stay strong, focused, and to speak up. When I talked to my sister Joline, she offered to take me to an Al-Anon meeting. Years ago, when she was married to an alcoholic, it had helped her.

Afraid the Al-Anon members would turn me away because Greg wasn't an alcoholic, I briefly explained my past with Bob and my current situation with Greg to the small group of nice people. They were very empathetic and told me I could stay. I only went to a few meetings, but it felt good to know that I had their support.

With continued focus and strength, our marriage began to thrive. I weaned myself off the anti-depressants.

The week after Halloween, Charlotte and Sherry came to Green Valley to help take care of me as I recovered from a scheduled hysterectomy. It gave the four us a chance to spend time talking. During their visit, Greg said something offensive. I can't remember what it was, but I do remember calling him on it, and his quick apology. In the past, it was something that I would have just swept under the rug, letting it fester.

It was Sherry's first visit to Green Valley, and she apologized for not coming sooner, but admitted that she had stayed away because of her anger towards Greg.

On Sunday morning, Greg and Sherry went to church while Charlotte stayed with me. When they arrived home, they were laughing. They explained to Charlotte and me how they felt the presence of God and his healing hand on them during the service. When they realized that they were the only two in the sanctuary sobbing, they both had the same thought: Obviously people were probably wondering what had brought up so much emotion between them. What if they thought they were mourning me—that something had gone wrong with my surgery.

We all laughed.

Chapter Five

Apple Pie

TWO DAYS BEFORE CHRISTMAS 2006, Greg and I arrived at Sherry's in Orange County for her birthday. The first year Greg and I were together, he suggested we bake a fresh apple pie on her birthday. Initially, I thought the pie was really about having a dessert to serve on Christmas Eve, when the rest of Greg's family would be gathered. But when 11-year-old Sherry said baking the pie was the favorite part of her birthday, it became our yearly tradition. The apple pie later also became symbolic of how harmoniously the three of us worked together at the office.

The coastal fog had lifted. I rang Sherry's doorbell while Greg hid behind the car holding two bags of Granny Smith apples.

"Happy birthday, sweetie, thirty-three years old. I can't believe it!" I shouted over the barking dogs.

Sherry reached out to hug me. "Oh, Mom it's so good to see you." Her shoulder-length sandy-blonde hair was tucked behind her ears. She wore a dress with "Winnie the Pooh" embroidered on the bodice. Such a childish look, I thought, compared to her perfectly applied lip-liner, her large diamond earrings, and the crisp scent of her perfume. I chuckled inside, that's my Sherry, such a fantasy buff. She could lose herself in the world of Harry Potter or The Lord of the Rings, but Disney was her favorite. Disney artwork hung on the walls of her family room and in her hallways.

We embraced long enough for Sherry to give me that extra squeeze like she'd always done. She was born with the knowledge of how to play the game of who loves who the most.

Then she craned her neck around my shoulder. "Where's Dad?"

On perfect cue, Greg popped up and came bounding across the driveway, extending one of the bags filled with apples to Sherry.

She smiled. "Awesome! I've got everything else ready to go." Then with a grin, she said, "Dad, I can't wait to show you the very cool apple peeler-corer I bought at William and Sonoma the other day. I've already tried it out, and it works perfectly!"

In Sherry's kitchen, the three of us took our positions like synchronized performers, waiting for the opening curtain call. Greg, like always, took the lead. He was the meticulous pastry chef who knew exactly how many drops of water to add depending upon on how much humidity was in the air. Through the years, Sherry had grown into the expert apple peeler and slicer. Her hands were petite but strong and steady. She squealed with delight as one continuous bright green strand of apple peel fell to the counter. And I was the stagehand, supporting Greg and Sherry. I sprinkled the mixture of sugar and cinnamon over the sliced apples. I wiped up the flour that covered the counters and dusted the floor, washed the dishes, and turned up the Christmas music. But mostly, I just watched the two of them.

Right before the pie was ready to go in the oven, Greg and Sherry stepped aside to give me the honor of crimping the upper and lower crusts together.

"No one can seal the deal like you," they said in unison. I blushed, secretly feeling like their hero.

Soon the aroma of baking apple pie filled the air. Greg and Sherry settled in at the kitchen table to play backgammon. The dogs hunted the kitchen tile for any morsel left behind.

I was so sure of myself, my marriage, and Greg's health. Everything was finally the way I had hoped it would be.

The next night, Christmas Eve, everyone lingered around the dining table, drinking wine and playing the cheap magic tricks that came out of the holiday poppers. In the kitchen, I snapped a photo of Greg and Sherry showing off the apple pie we'd baked, Greg in his red plaid shirt and Sherry in her Christmas sweater. Both smiling.

Greg sliced. Sherry and I served the big pieces, not knowing this would be the last pie we'd bake together.

Chapter Six

Flash of Light

TWO DAYS AFTER CHRISTMAS, a tall woman with jet-black hair walked in behind the curtained area of the ER at Scripps Hospital. She extended her hand to Greg. "Hello, I'm Dr. Knight."

Greg shook her hand and cleared his throat. "I'm Greg Hayes....Dr. Hayes, a retired dentist." He was still a stickler about letting people know how to address him. Even after retiring, he asked his golfing buddies to call him "Doc" instead of Greg.

"What brings you in this morning?"

Greg answered. "I saw a flash of light during Christmas Eve dinner...perhaps a mini-stroke?"

Of course he saw a flash of light. There was light everywhere...the chandelier, the candles, and the twinkling Christmas lights. Greg and I both knew the importance of being seen right away whenever a stroke is suspected, so I was confused about why he'd waited 48 hours to say anything.

On the 26th, we said our good-byes to Sherry, Chris, and the dogs. Greg battled the holiday traffic on I-5 as we headed south to housesit for some friends. When he pulled into our friend's driveway, he turned toward me and casually mentioned that he might have had a stroke on Christmas Eve, but insisted he was fine. I let it go. I trusted his knowledge. If it was anything serious, wouldn't he have asked me to drive?

"Any headache?" Dr. Knight asked.

"Not now...but I had one yesterday." Yes, I thought to myself, he did ask me for Advil. That was easily explained, since we'd slept on Sherry's uncomfortable guest bed.

I glanced over at Greg's sister, Bev. Through the years, whenever I got frustrated and angry at her brother, she understood. She would comfort me and continue to love Greg—exactly what I needed her to do. She had stopped by to pick up a scarf she had left behind and insisted that we go to the ER after I told her what Greg had said the night before.

Greg was always proactive about his health, but still I thought he would resist his sister's insistence. When he agreed to go, I still wasn't alarmed. In fact, while driving to the hospital, I thought, *we'll be back in an hour or so.* He had no pain, no fever, and no cancer.

Greg explained his cancer history to Dr. Knight.

"You seem to be somewhat slow in your responses," Dr. Knight said. *What's she talking about? He answered everything. He didn't skip a beat.* I nudged Bev, giving her the eye: *Don't worry, we'll be out of here before you know it.*

Dr. Knight pulled back the curtain. "I'm ordering a brain scan."

Bev and I grabbed each other's hand. A nurse came in and quickly explained that an ambulance would transport Greg across the parking lot for the MRI.

"Can I go with him?"

The nurse answered no and rolled my husband away.

Bev walked out into the hallway to call her parents. I figured I should go move the car out of the temporary spot. But once inside the car, I couldn't move. I felt like I was in a straightjacket. I watched the ambulance snake its way across the huge parking lot. I had to pull myself together. I wiped my tears. I needed to call Sherry and Charlotte. *Dear God, don't let my world fall apart. Not now. We've come so far.*

"Mom, I can leave right now," Sherry said.

"Ok. But I'm sure he's fine," I whispered.

Charlotte and Stuart had left earlier that morning to go visit friends in Tahoe. "We just reached the California-

Nevada border," Charlotte said. "We can turn around and come back."

"Oh, honey, that's a long drive. I'll call you back when I know more."

Feeling more grounded knowing Sherry would be coming soon, I parked the car and went back inside to meet up with Bev. Within minutes, we saw the nurse rolling the gurney toward us—Greg waving.

In the next breath, the three of us were back behind the curtain listening to Dr. Knight.

"I'm sorry. You have a brain tumor," she said, handing Greg the written report and scan.

What does all this mean? The only thing I was able to absorb were the tears streaming down Greg's and Bev's cheeks. *Why were they so upset? Did I miss something?*

I leaned over to get a better look at the image. *Oh my God, it looks like it's taking up a quarter of his brain.* I scanned the report: 3cm lesion in the right frontal lobe…surrounded by significant swelling. Second lesion in the right temporal area measuring 10mm and a mass effect in the right lateral ventricle. My jaw tightened, eyes narrowing as I attempted to understand. All I could see was the huge mass.

Within minutes, the medical director of the Intensive Care Unit, Dr. Eisman, came in. He looked at Greg, "We need to get you into ICU. Until we can decide what to do for you."

Greg glanced down at his IV. He looked at me, then closed his eyes and took a deep breath. "Steroids. The drug doctors love and hate."

"Why?" I asked.

"Reduces the swelling, but can have bad side effects." He always knew the answer to every question I ever had.

It was getting late. I felt so helpless. Doctors kept coming in handing me their business cards. The waiting room outside the ICU was now filled with family and friends. Charlotte and Stuart had come back anyway. I couldn't bear to leave Greg.

"We don't allow anyone to stay overnight in ICU," the nurse said. Greg's parents insisted that I go home with them to get some sleep. I reluctantly agreed.

The doctors and nurses had moved so fast. Now, in ICU, everything stood still. They couldn't figure out what to do with Greg.

We never returned to Arizona. We decided to stay in Southern California to treat Greg's cancer.

Chapter Seven

Cancer, Sweetie, Cancer

CANCER TREATMENT TENDS TO make everything else in your life disappear, or at least diminish in importance, but for Greg and me, nothing could take away our gratitude. In spite of the state of his health—which was not good—we healed our hearts, our spirit, and our marriage.

Greg never apologized for his prior abusive behavior, but he thanked me every day, and he wrote me a letter:

My Dearest Rhonda,

There are so many wonderful features about you that I want to take a few minutes and simply thank you for them. Thank you for being my wife, lover, and soul mate. I am just becoming aware of how grateful I am to have you in my life. I am especially grateful for your guidance in spirituality. Thank you for challenging me to find my spiritual side. Thank you for including me in your life. Your tenderness and devotion was what got me through this difficult time and allowed me to open up to the perfect healing that God gave us.

Together, we thanked God every night.

After Greg recovered from the brain surgery, we spent every other week in the hospital while he was infused with a high-dose chemo drug called methotrexate, only to find out several months later that his brain tumor was still growing. It was devastating news. But miraculously, once radiation treatments began, they did the trick, and Greg slowly regained his strength.

While Greg and I were getting settled into our new place, Sherry occasionally mentioned having sporadic stomach pains. None of us thought much of it. She was working hard as a dental hygienist and was under a lot of stress. She had previously complained of joint pain, too, but that had gone away — or so she said. Sherry was keeping a log of what she ate, to see if she could narrow it down to a particular food.

Sometimes I would go up to visit Sherry and watch her quilt, cross-stitch, or bake cookies. Her hands were never idle. I talked to her about my fears over Greg dying, and she would nod, assuring me that if and when it happened, she would be there to comfort me. Charlotte did that, too, whenever we talked on the phone, but she was immersed in her teaching career and PhD program. It was more realistic to think that my comfort would come from Sherry. She had that natural motherly instinct and only lived an hour away.

Six months after Greg's brain tumor diagnosis, Sherry and Chris returned from a Baltic cruise. Sherry called and said that Chris had taken her to the ER because she had some rectal bleeding. She laughed it off, thinking it was from all the travel, but when the doctor saw a blockage in her colon on the abdominal X-ray, they admitted her. Greg insisted I go stay with Sherry, assuring me he'd call his parents or sister if he needed anything. When I arrived at Mission Hospital, Sherry was getting settled into a room and didn't seem to be the least bit nervous about the colonoscopy she'd be having the first thing in the morning. Chris went home, and I stayed with her. Before we turned out the lights, a soft-spoken doctor came in. Sherry had obviously already met him.

She pointed towards me, saying, "Dr. Feng, this is my mom."

I leaned forward to shake his hand.

He said, "Would you like to see Sherry's X-ray?"

It took me a moment to respond—certainly this couldn't be serious. "Sure," I said.

I followed him past the nurses' station to a small area with a desk, an X-ray view box, and a computer.

Dr. Feng put the film on the screen and clicked it on pointing to the X-ray he said, "I wanted you to see this before tomorrow's procedure."

He continued. "Here's the blockage in her colon. Then he pointed to a different part of the X-ray. "This is the lower part of her lungs. This is really what concerns me."

I looked at the speckled areas, not understanding.

Her lungs? What could be wrong with her lungs? She's having stomach pain, bleeding. For a second, I was confused. Then I realized I'd seen this before.

Breathe.

"My husband has brain cancer." *Surely, if he knows about Greg, he couldn't tell me that anything was seriously wrong with Sherry.*

Dr. Feng placed his hand on my shoulder. "I've heard about your husband. I'm sorry."

I massaged my temples, trying to make it all go away. Then I pulled myself up. I was over-reacting. After all, Sherry wasn't concerned, and Chris had gone home. I thanked Dr. Feng and walked back to the hospital room. I held Sherry all night.

The following morning, the Fourth of July, I walked alongside the gurney while the nurse wheeled Sherry through the quiet halls. We stopped at the closed door. The black sign read: Gastroenterology. I kissed Sherry on the forehead. Dr. Feng came out and directed me across the hallway to a small waiting room, then followed Sherry into the OR.

Dr. Feng came back much sooner than I expected. I could see the bad news in his face.

"I'm so sorry," he said, "It certainly looks like cancer. Of course, we need to get the final lab results. Her lungs, well, we need to confirm that, too."

I felt the familiar rush of adrenaline. "Oh no," I gasped. In that instant I felt like I had been sucked up in a vacuum and then abruptly spewed out. Everything vanished from my mind except for my old chant: God is with me, I am at peace. I wasn't at peace, but it was the prayer I turned to.

In the recovery area, I brushed Sherry's sandy-blonde hair away from her ear and whispered, "Sherry, I'm here."

She stirred and wanted to know what they had found.

"Was it just gas pain? Hemorrhoids?" she asked.

I told myself—be strong, be the mom, be the grown-up. But, honestly, all I wanted to do was cry. I took another breath. She wanted the truth, and it was my job to give it to her.

"Cancer, sweetie, cancer."

"Cancer?" she said, "I...I never thought."

"Oh, honey...."

How frustrated she had been for the past year, first with the joint pain, then her stomach. None of it made sense. At one point, her doctor said maybe it was fibromyalgia.

Had Sherry given up on finding an answer? I felt so guilty. I should have pushed her to keep looking. But when she quit complaining, I thought she was better. Now I wondered if she'd quit talking about her pain because of

Greg's condition. After working all day, she would fight the traffic, for hours, to come visit Greg in the hospital. She always arrived with a smile. Sometimes she'd sing to him. Other times, she sat quietly, gently stroking the top of his hand while he was being infused with chemo. *How could I have missed that she was hurting?*

Unlike me, Sherry had always been brave about pain. When she was ten, she waited a week before telling me about her collarbone. It was right after Greg and I had started dating. One day at the pool, she began to cry for no apparent reason. Tears fell as she stood, swimsuit dripping, and said, "Mom, I've got to tell you now."

I had no idea what could possibly be bothering her. "What, sweetie?"

"It was a dumb thing to do."

A week earlier she had fallen trying to do a cartwheel while wearing a pair of boxing gloves. Knowing we had no health insurance, Sherry didn't want to add to my burdens. She'd been living with the pain of the fractured collarbone for a week. After I took her to the doctor, the only thing that helped relieve my guilt was when he said there was no treatment. He could give her a brace to wear, but there was nothing else to be done. That day, I made Sherry promise she'd never keep anything like that from me again.

"Cancer?" Then with a sigh she said, "Well at least I haven't lost my mind. Mom, don't you worry. Where's Chris?"

I was already irritated that Chris hadn't arrived yet. I understood he was tired from their recent traveling in Europe and from being with her in the ER the day before. But I certainly thought that he would be back before they took her in for the colonoscopy. He knew it would be the first thing in the morning.

"On his way," I said, although I had no idea if he was or not.

I scolded myself for being so hard on Chris, because Sherry didn't seem to be annoyed, just curious. Then I couldn't hold back any longer. "Sherry, I need to know. Are you happy? Your life, your marriage. Do you need anything? I promise I'll do anything you want."

"I'm happy. All I want is to go home, be with Chris and the girls." "Girls" is what Sherry called her Yorkies.

Then she stroked the top of my hand as tears rolled down her cheeks. "Mom, I don't know what I'd do without you," she said.

I wiped her tears as my own fell. I didn't know what I'd do without her. My younger daughter, the old soul.

I wanted to believe that Sherry could live with cancer. She was healthy and strong at thirty-three. Disney movies and characters were still her favorite things. She didn't even have crow's feet yet. But we learned her cancer was Stage IV. It had already spread from her colon to both lungs.

Two weeks after surgery, the day Sherry was dismissed from the hospital, the oncologist told us they would "manage" her cancer as long as possible. There would be no cure. So Sherry went home to be with Chris and her Yorkies.

I went home to be with Greg. Each night, I lay there wondering what was coming next.

Chapter Eight

Questions for God

MY SPIRITUAL LIFE WAS always a mixed blessing. Growing up, I had the freedom to believe anything I wanted. In my younger years, I learned about Jesus, Paramahansa Yogananda, meditation, and yoga from my mother's friends George and Doris. As I grew older, I would ask kids at school or people in my neighborhood to invite me to their church— and they usually did. For weeks, sometimes months, I would do my best to pray like they prayed and believe in what they believed in, but it never completely worked out. Should I get down on my knees and press my palms together? Should I sweep my hand across my forehead and chest in the sign of the cross? Or should I raise my hands up to the sky and speak in tongues? I wasn't sure.

The only thing I was sure of—for as long as I could remember—was that I felt the spirit of God within me. I would just talk to him, in my mind, like he was a friend. A very smart friend who knew it all. I believed that someday God would reveal his plan to me, but I wasn't sure when or what his plan would be.

For a while, we worked out a new kind of normal. Greg and I continued to get settled into our townhome and took a Fall Color Cruise with his parents. Sherry returned to work and was coping with the side effects of the chemo. Despite all that, I could never quite let go of one fear: What would I do if both Greg and Sherry needed me at the same time?

Other family members and friends could help, and that was okay. Still, I wanted to be there for both of them. It brought me comfort to fluff their pillows, stroke their hands, and make sure they were taken care of. Anyone suffering from a serious illness deserved a dedicated advocate— someone to question the doctors, watch the nurses, research the Internet, to keep medications and appointments straight. I thought about all the sick people who didn't have anyone to help them, and how scary that must be.

I had not been able to be with my sick mother. The first year Greg and I were married, when she was diagnosed with colon cancer, I was in California, running the practice, raising my kids, going to college, and being a wife. She was in Tucson. Twenty years later, after she died, I still felt guilty that I hadn't done more for her.

Distressed about Greg's and Sherry's health, the outlook was grim for them both, still, I knew I could make a difference, and I was grateful for that. I just prayed my fear of needing to care for them both simultaneously didn't become a reality.

Late one night as we lay in bed, Greg asked, "Will you do something for me?"

I turned toward him. "Of course. What?"

"Visualize that I'm gone."

I knew exactly what he meant. He often talked about the power of visualization. He used it when he played golf. He used it to try to shrink his brain tumors. When Sherry was in the hospital, one of her nurses came in wearing a smock with colorful fish. Greg told everyone to visualize the fish swallowing up Sherry's tumors. He even sent an email out to everyone we knew requesting that they do the same.

I slowly rolled over to my back. My eyes wide open. "Okay."

The moonlight cast a shadow on the bedroom wall, illuminating the heating duct register high on the wall. I focused on that register and did my best to imagine that Greg wasn't in bed with me.

"What will you do?" he whispered.

A few days earlier, we had talked with our pastor about having a celebration instead of a funeral for Greg.

I said, "First I'll have your Celebration of Life." I paused. Greg was silent.

"Then I'll go take care of Sherry." I closed my eyes. "Then I'll start *Help Me, Rhonda*."

"Good—I like your strength," he said. He touched my shoulder and continued. "You know you've got to get out…have fun."

I didn't want to keep playing his game of Zen, but I wanted to please him, make him proud of me, like always. I said, "I know, but…what if something comes up that we haven't talked about…."

"Don't worry. If we haven't talked about it, it's not important, at least not to me. Follow your heart and do whatever you want," he said. "You can get married again."

"Thank you," I whispered into the darkness.

In early February, Greg's radiation oncologist, Dr. Linson, told us that Greg's brain tumors would keep springing up like leaks in a garden hose—patch one and another one would burst open. This put the whole family on alert. Charlotte drove over from Phoenix for another visit.

When she arrived, she dropped her suitcase at the front door and said, "I'm exhausted. Between work and my dissertation, I've been working around the clock."

I clenched my jaw tight. I always admired her for knowing exactly what career path she wanted to take, but I didn't need her to show up to tell me how tired she was. I pulled her aside and whispered, "You are so selfish. Your dad and Sherry are dying and you have the nerve to show up and complain about how tired you are."

"I'm sorry, Mom. But yes, I am tired." She adjusted the clip holding her long blonde hair. "The traveling back and forth makes it even harder, but I'm here now."

"You can be tired now, but when they're gone, I'm going to need you."

I knew I was being unfair. But I wanted to fix everything in one conversation, to have Charlotte say, "Of course, Mom, I'll drop everything and come be with you." But how could she have responded that way to my tirade? She went back home without saying a thing, but surely she was hurt and angry.

I later called to apologize, relieved when she said, "Mom, I understand. You don't owe me an apology. I love you."

The following week Greg got the news we expected: another tumor had grown. Greg held me in his arms and sobbed. "Honey, the hardest part about dying is that I'm going to miss you so damn much."

I choked up. I wrote his words down each time he did or said something endearing. How much comfort I got later from those scribbled notes.

The size and location of a brain tumor produces a variety of symptoms. One of Greg's was weakness on his left side. Each day, his gait worsened. My biggest concern was for his safety, so I bought him a cane at the drug store. It was one of those stainless steel ones with holes and pegs allowing for height adjustments.

He sat in the recliner for hours, counting the nine holes. The tip of his forefinger touching each hole square-on and the whisper from his lips, one...two...three. Then he'd hold it up like a rifle, pointing the rubber tip straight out into the room, peering through the imaginary scope. It was a little unsettling to see him do that; he'd always been anti-guns. I wondered what he was thinking and feeling. Yet, I never sensed he was angry or frustrated, so I just let him be.

I became more and more sleep-deprived, worrying about his safety, even with the help of the cane. Early one morning, I was awakened by a big crash. Greg had fallen in the shower—again. I knew I had to come up with a safer plan. That night, after getting into bed, I pinned one end of a long piece of elastic to his pajamas. He gave me an inquisitive look—*Are we playing a new game?* I secured the other end of the elastic to my nightgown and smiled. "So you won't get away from me."

He grinned wide and said, "Who in their right mind would want to get away from you?"

We laughed and hugged.

Tethered together, I slept like a baby.

One morning in late February, I was dazed when I noticed an open document on the task bar of my laptop entitled "Greg's Final Wishes." The first five words read: *I am ready to go.* I didn't want him to be ready to go; I wanted him to stay with me.

For the past fourteen months, we had prepared for all of this. He wanted an open casket and then cremation. He wanted me to wear a piece of jewelry close to my heart that contained a part of his ashes, and to scatter some on the golf course. He wanted to have all happy, upbeat '60s songs at his Celebration of Life.

As I continued to read, it was reassuring that I knew all of his wishes, but impossible to hold back my tears when I reached the part about "our song." He wrote:

The one song that must definitely be played is "You Are" by Lionel Ritchie. I will be present in my family's heart for the occasion, so be happy for all I have had the pleasure to enjoy and know that I have no regrets. I hope I have challenged you all to be the best you can be and to BE HAPPY.

I worried that if he was *ready to go* and had actually written down his final wishes that he would actually die sooner than I had imagined. I watched every move he made, fearing that the final event could happen any second, but after only a few weeks of radiation treatments, the tumor had shrunk.

Feeling stronger, and no longer needing his cane, Greg was ready to travel. In one afternoon, he made hotel reservations and travel arrangements. In the span of six weeks, there would first be a weekend trip to Palm Springs to celebrate his parents' 60th wedding anniversary. The following weekend would be a drive over to Phoenix for Charlotte's Carpe Diem party to celebrate her PhD. Then two weeks in Hawaii and on to Washington DC to visit Greg's son. Even in the healthiest of times all this travel would have concerned me—I hated to pack—and now I worried about Greg developing another brain tumor and about being so far away from Sherry. But how could I say no?

The first weekend in May, minutes after Greg and I arrived at the hotel in Palm Springs, Sherry called. Her latest CT scan results were in.

"Mom...my lungs...the tumors have doubled," she said, her voice quivering.

My stomach tightened. "Oh..., sweetie."

"The chemo's not working." She sobbed.

I paced in the lobby. "The new drugs will work," I said, to reassure both of us.

I told myself this wasn't an emergency. We had come to Palm Springs for a big celebration for Greg's parents and family. They had moved it up—almost four months earlier than the actual date—so Greg wouldn't miss it. I didn't want to ruin their celebration. I knew, if needed, I could be by Sherry's side in two hours.

She coughed. "My chest hurts."

The mere thought of her chest hurting made mine feel like it had exploded. I couldn't stand the thought of Sherry, the daughter who always mothered me, crying out in pain.

She was the four-year-old who stopped playing with her dolls to put her arms around me when she sensed I was having a bad day. She was the nine-year-old who kissed me to thank me for her birthday present. She was the sixteen-year-old who held my hand at the mall simply because she loved me.

I took in a deep breath, hoping she would do the same. "Everything's gonna be alright, honey." I wanted her to believe it so I could, too.

Sherry sighed. "I know. I don't know what I'd do without you, Mom. You always know how to make me feel better."

Relieved, I said, again, "If you need me, remember, I can be there in two hours."

I turned my attention back to Greg, who had taken a seat to rest. He looked so different with the mustache that he had recently grown to avert the eye away from the long dented scar on the top of his bald head. But his biggest change was on the inside. At first, I wondered if Greg's spiritual awakening was a mere side-effect of the tumors. But now I knew he had truly found his way. Since that day in Green Valley, he prayed and meditated daily. He even told me that he hoped to purify himself enough to become an angel. In my mind, he had already achieved that. He exuded love and compassion.

Before I walked over to tell Greg the news about Sherry, I took a moment to draw in his energy. Then I felt a lump rise in my throat. My thoughts darted back and forth. Who needed me more—my husband or daughter?

I chose to stay with Greg and his family, but later that

night in the hotel room it was impossible to sleep. *I panicked at the possibility of them both dying on the same day.*

Sherry said her chest hurt, but I hadn't gone to her. How disappointed Greg would be if we didn't go to Hawaii. But I knew I couldn't.

I leaned into Greg's chest and whispered into the dark. "I can't, sweetheart. I can't go to Hawaii with you."

Greg touched my lips. "I know," he whispered back.

In the silence and understanding, I needed him more than I needed Sherry. He would be the one to soothe my grief over losing her. He'd understand. He would be the water to my fire.

But how could I place a value on who went first, based on my own selfish reasons? Despite my guilt, I pleaded to God, if you are going to take them both, at least let me choose who goes first. Apologizing, I buried my sobs in the pillow.

All my fears about traveling were for nothing, because together we worked it all out. God, once again, proved to me that he was watching out for us all. The following weekend, Greg, Sherry, and I drove to Phoenix for Charlotte's PhD celebration. Sherry and I baked and decorated cupcakes. Greg was the videographer. He walked around with his new camcorder filming family and friends' congratulations for Charlotte.

Greg convinced his golfing buddy, Vern, to join him the first week in Hawaii. His parents joined him for the second. I stayed home with Sherry, which helped to improve her health and spirits.

While unpacking Greg's suitcase after he returned from Kauai, I found a yellow legal pad on top of his clothes. He had always kept some kind of a journal log whenever we traveled. I sat at the foot of the bed reading the entries, relieved he had felt well enough to write. He wrote about the details of golf and his meals. He mentioned volcano ash that had blanketed most of the island, and how he feared it would be a disappointment to Vern. He wrote about Vern's kindness for buying a bottle of Absolute vodka as a welcome gift for Greg's parents when they arrived. The original plan was that Greg would spend a few hours alone after Vern's flight departed and before his parents arrived. However, his parents' flight was cancelled, and Greg spent more than 24 hours alone. I flipped to the next page, which had obviously been written during that time frame:

I find myself isolated on an island paradise with time for spiritual reading and reflection. My personal journey since Christmas Eve 2006 has been an emotional rollercoaster which now only eighteen months later has settled down and allowed me time for introspection. All the positives were attainable only through love and I am so blessed to have a spouse who emulates love. Up until about two years ago, I did not have a clue what love meant, and when Rhonda threatened to leave me it was time for me to take a hard look at myself and accept my role in the relationship issues. So, I read all that I could to seek a path of self-improvement. It paid off big time as Rhonda stayed with me, perceiving the effort I was making and, thanks to God, she was there and remained by my side through the terrible ordeal of cancer. I suppose I am writing this more for me than you. After all, I may never even know if you read it or just tossed it away. But you must understand that you may never get a second chance, so now is the time to give your heart to your spouse.

It wasn't addressed to anyone in particular. I was deeply touched by the tender words he wrote about what we had been through, but more so by the fact that he seemed to want to help someone else.

Three days later we flew to Washington, DC, to visit his son Michael, daughter-in-law, and grandson. Unfortunately, Greg became very weak during the final days of that trip. As soon as we returned home, we learned a new tumor had sprung up on Greg's brain-stem, the center of life.

One way or another, I had to accept the reality that God's plan wasn't for Greg to help me through my grief over losing Sherry. I was saddened beyond belief, but grateful that all of Greg's wishes in life had been fulfilled. When we talked about that fact, however, Greg surprised me. He had one more thing that he wanted to do. He wanted to hear me give a speech at Toastmasters.

I had joined Toastmasters about ten months earlier to help overcome my deathly fear of public speaking. For years I had talked about joining, and Greg encouraged me to do it. Since we lived right down the street from where the meetings were held, I gave it a try. However, between all the hospital stays with Greg and Sherry, I wasn't able to make it to many meetings. I gave two speeches, though, surprised at how much I enjoyed it. In the back of my mind, I thought I could very easily become a motivational speaker. I wanted to share our story. Help people realize that it's important to address issues they may have in their relationships. Greg and I were so grateful that we had figured out what was wrong with our marriage, *before* he was diagnosed. We both knew that, if we hadn't had this blessing, Greg's illness and the end of his life would have been so much more difficult. We considered it to be miraculous and certainly thanked God every night for it. For me, as a caregiver, it was a blessing to feel totally loved and appreciated. For Greg, as a dying man, it was a blessing for him to be at peace with me, himself, and God.

What would I speak about with Greg there? Of course, I wanted to shout it out from the rooftop how grateful we were that we had renewed our love. We believed that mailing the letter was the key to our success—the intervention. Even when I had shown it to Dr. Julie, my counselor, she was impressed. She invited me to come to a women's retreat that she was holding so I could read it to the group. When I asked Greg what he thought about me giving a speech encouraging others to heal their relationships before it was too late, tell them about the letter and intervention, he agreed.

I titled my speech "The Letter." I practiced in front of Greg, ten or more times, until I could make it all the way through without crying. When we arrived at the Toastmasters meeting on the appointed night, I felt the butterflies build up in my stomach. I wondered what people would think about me sharing our personal story. I turned toward Greg. "Are you sure?"

Greg reached for the car's handle. "Yes," he said quickly. Then he looked at me. "Please, it needs to be heard."

Even though we had talked so many times about the value in sharing our experience, this was my final confirmation.

When we entered the room, I introduced Greg to a few of the members, but he wasn't able to hold much of a conversation with a stranger. He just smiled. He hooked his cane on the back of his seat, the one closest to the podium, then he leaned in and said, "I love you. I'm so proud."

With everyone seated and quiet, I stood behind the podium, notes in hand, and began.

"Two years ago I was hopeless, desperate, and spiritless, with nowhere else to turn. My husband Greg and I had been married for over twenty years, and I wanted to pack my bags and leave." I paused and took a breath. "Instead, I turned to God, wrote a letter and mailed it." I explained how elephants exist in families, but some people don't have the courage to stand up to them. I talked about the courage it took for me to mail the letter and how it ended up being the defining moment, the miracle of our marriage. I told them Greg had been diagnosed with his sixth brain tumor, and the diagnosis wasn't good, but despite all of the bad news, the good news was that we had filled our lives, our marriage, with light and love. The meeting was in the cafeteria of the Salvation Army, but now it felt like we were in St. Stephen's Cathedral. I scanned the room, saw light and love in everyone's face, especially Greg's.

"Before it's too late, do whatever you need to do to make things right in a relationship. Have faith, listen to your deepest inner voice, and you will do the right thing." I smiled, extended my arm out, and said, "Mr. Toastmaster."

A few days later, Greg's family and a few close friends gathered to celebrate his last birthday. His body was weary, but his spirit was lively. We all wore birthday hats and blew on birthday whistles. Sherry pinned a birthday-boy badge on his T-shirt. During the party, one of our friends, Terri, was taking pictures. She went upstairs to get a shot from the loft, while Greg, Sherry, Charlotte, and I embraced. We all looked up and smiled. Our last picture as a family.

Greg's decline came quickly after the party. He chose to stay at home, with the help of hospice. A hospital bed and wheelchair arrived on the morning that Greg's daughter Kimberly flew down from Seattle to say her final good-bye. A few days later, a hospice nurse came and began to administer morphine. Greg stopped eating and speaking. His body grew even thinner.

When Greg's breathing changed to a deep rattling rasp, I called everyone. Charlotte decided not to come back, since she had already said her good-bye when we celebrated Greg's birthday, and I understood that decision.

Between my sisters and Greg's family, I had a house full of helpers. I was so grateful.

I hoped Sherry would feel the same as Charlotte. I

wanted her to stay home to rest. She had quit working several months earlier, due to her coughing and the neuropathy in her hands. But she insisted on coming.

On August 16, 2008, eleven days after Greg's fifty-ninth birthday, at two in the afternoon, he let out one last trembling breath. I stood numbly at his bedside, Sherry slipping one arm around my waist. Her touch felt so good. But as I watched Greg's mother sob on his father's shoulder, it was a painful reminder of how I had begged God to give me Greg to help me grieve Sherry. How would I survive losing her, too?

Then I heard Sherry say, "Dad, I'll see you soon."

For the next several hours, I lay next to Greg, whispering good-byes, Sherry's words echoing in my mind.

Then, I heard a voice deep within me say, "Get up now! Go be strong for Sherry! Be happy and enjoy the time you have left with her."

Chapter Nine

Changes

GREG'S CELEBRATION OF LIFE was just what he'd wanted. His family and friends witnessed him in the casket, because he believed this was the quickest way for everyone to face the reality of his death. He wanted everyone to acknowledge his passing, then get on with living.

I wore a straight black skirt, and a tailored black and gold top. I usually wore long, flowing dresses, but when my sister-in-law Bev and I had gone shopping for outfits, she picked it out and said it was appropriate. It didn't matter what I wore, I thought, because nothing would ever be appropriate or normal again.

I arrived early at the funeral home. Stepping into the room where Greg's service would be held, I sobbed when I saw him lying there in the casket. But when I heard "All You Need Is Love" playing, my crying abruptly stopped. Greg wanted all upbeat songs from the '60s—from the Beatles to Led Zeppelin. The music helped take me from mourning to rejoicing in him. Gratitude filled me as family, friends, patients, and past employees—some we hadn't seen for years—filled the large funeral chapel to standing room only. Many people spoke lovingly about the impact Greg had on their lives. Charlotte addressed the crowd, telling them how Greg had taught her the importance of staying disciplined and following her passion in life. I laughed when Sherry told the story of how impressed she was when Greg had shown up wearing a tie on our first date. She talked openly about her disease and how she and Greg had become cancer buddies. When Kimberly spoke about the first few years of her life, and Michael spoke about the summer vacations, I felt saddened that they didn't have more time to spend with their father.

The day after the service, Charlotte and Stuart had to go home to get back to work. Sherry and I laid out our plans to support each other. We agreed that I would stay with her all week, take her to chemo, and then go back to my house on

Chris's day off. It sounded like a healthy balance. We would have plenty of time together, and I could ease myself into being alone, something that I had never been good at. In all our years together, Greg rarely went out of town without me or out alone for an evening, but whenever he did I would be fine until the sun began to set. Then I would become scared, close every blind, and turn every light on. I imagined a peeping tom or an ax murderer lurking outside on the porch. That's the main reason why Greg and I had chosen to live in a 55+ retirement community with a gate-guarded security staff after we moved back to Southern California. He had a fatal disease, and we knew the day would come when I would be alone. Now that day was here—and I couldn't bear the thought of a long stretch of nights alone.

As soon as all the other out-of-town family and friends left to get back to their lives, I packed up my car with my pillows, clothes, paperwork, laptop, and Greg's urn, to go spend my first five days at Sherry's.

Before I left Oceanside, I had to stop at the bank to sign some paperwork. The form had only two options: married or single. I was surprised that I didn't also see *divorced* or *widowed,* like I'd seen on other documents.

"I'm not sure which box to check," I said to the young girl sitting across the desk. She looked at me with a blank stare, so I went on to explain. "I'm married, but my husband…. I'm widowed." I had never given any thought to the word *widowed* before, but now that I used it to describe myself, it repulsed me. I felt old and pitiful, and I didn't have time for that. I had to take care of Sherry.

The girl flipped her long brunette hair over her shoulder. "Check single."

This wasn't going to be easy. I checked married.

Before I reached my car, my phone rang. It was Sherry.

I took a deep breath and did my best to sound cheerful. I wasn't going to burden her with my life. "Hi, sweetie."

"Hi, Mom…. On your way?"

"I'm leaving the bank now. I'll be there in an hour."

"Good. Love you."

I half-smiled. "Love you, too." I couldn't wait to see her.

Less than a month later, the doctor's last-ditch effort to manage Sherry's cancer with weekly chemo was proving futile. Our only hope now was to get her accepted into a clinical trial—in other words, we couldn't do anything other than keep ourselves as busy as possible while we sat around and waited.

At first, Sherry and I went to a few cancer support group meetings, because we figured that's what people in our situation do. I even scheduled an individual grief counseling session for the same reason. The most helpful information I got was when the counselor explained to me that grief was different for everyone. Sherry and I concluded that we needed to do something different, something positive that helped others.

We explored getting Rose and Olivia certified as pet

therapy dogs, but they didn't qualify. Before we knew it, our days were filled with not doing much of anything. We played Monopoly, backgammon, and hearts. We searched for the same jig saw piece. She taught me how to feed the dogs by tossing their pellets of food across the floor. I wondered how they would survive without her and thought about what a good mother she would've been. I watched her nap, breathe, and smile. I laughed and cried with her, and marveled at her beauty. She talked about her childhood memories of monkey bars, mac-n-cheese, her dog Peanut, and how she and her sister played school. She was always the student and Charlotte the teacher. Our conversations would always come back to our loving and missing Greg, how amazing it was that he finally learned how to love.

In mid-October, my sister Diana came out for a visit and suggested, since we weren't doing anything else, that we should all plan a trip to Disney World. Sherry and Chris had yearly passes to Disneyland and frequently visited. Sherry had always dreamed about going to Disney World, but didn't think it would ever happen. So the week before Thanksgiving, despite Sherry's coughing, lack of oxygen, and pain from six cracked ribs, Chris, Sherry, and I headed off to Florida to meet Diana and her husband Jody. Sherry never showed any lack of energy, and now she was able to zip around in a rented wheelchair.

Minutes before the first Christmas lighting of Cinderella's Castle, Sherry got out of the wheelchair and wrapped her arms around me. Even though we were surrounded by a huge crowd, it was as if we were the only ones there. Neither of us spoke a word, but I could tell by the squeeze of her hand that we were thinking the same thing as the lights magically popped on: *The castle had been lit up just for us.*

The following evening, after another long day of walking, shopping, and riding roller coasters, I went out to soak in the hotel's hot tub. I struck up a conversation with the only other person who was there, a man. He was attentive when I told him all about Sherry and how we had traveled so far. He nodded with understanding when I told him how lonely I was without Greg. After a short while he smiled and said, "Hey, do you want to go down the waterslide?" I wasn't sure what I should do, so I acted way braver than I felt and said, "Sure!"

We jumped out of the hot water and ran up the stairs that wound through lush greenery to the top of the slide. Catching my breath and laughing, I insisted that he go first to show me the way. I hadn't been down a waterslide in years. I followed not too far behind him, my pulse pounding. As my momentum picked up, I began to feel like a kid; I held my arms up in the air and hooted and hollered. When I hit the cool water and saw this nice gentleman waiting for me, I felt a glimmer of hope. I looked up to the sky recalling the conversation that Greg and I had that night in bed when he wanted me to visualize that he was gone. Maybe I could be attracted to someone again, and someone could feel the same for me. And as soon the thought came to me, it was almost as if he had read my mind. He looked me straight in the eye and said, "I'm married." We parted ways.

I'm not sure if that's what got me noticing wedding rings, but after that I always looked at men's and women's ring-fingers. My wedding ring wasn't just a symbol of my marriage to Greg. It was a single band with three small diamonds surrounded by two rows of littler ones. Beautiful and comfortable, it was a part of me. I had shopped for it by myself. When I took Greg to see it, he agreed and bought it. So I continued to wear it. Yet, I couldn't help but feel a pang of jealousy when I saw someone else's wedding band, which I knew was ridiculous and selfish. After all, even wearing a ring, they too could be aching from loneliness.

With each passing week, every time I'd load up Greg's urn and all the rest of my things to go back home for my two nights, I dreaded it more. The gates and guards calmed my fears, but couldn't alleviate my profound loneliness.

In the early years of our marriage, I'd get tired of the Sports Channel. Greg would listen to one game on the radio while flipping back and forth between games on the TV: football, tennis, ice hockey, basketball, baseball, golf. I eventually learned how to tune it out, but now the silence was deafening. In our bedroom, I turned on the golf channel. I then went into the living room to watch HGTV, keeping the volume down low enough so I could hear the other TV, pretending Greg was still there. This couldn't go on forever.

No matter how much I pretended, anxiety rose in me as the sun dipped lower into the sky. And then the dreaded dinner time came. Even though I knew it was ridiculous, I set the table for two and lit the candles. From the kitchen, I yelled, "Greg, dinner's ready!" At the table, I gave thanks, then poured myself a glass of wine.

The excruciating loneliness stayed for several hours, then came back in the middle of the night.

Early in December, on one of my nights at home alone, I stopped by the grocery store to get something for dinner. A woman who appeared to be in her early seventies was in the frozen food section looking at the same individual serving dinners. After spotting her ring-less finger, I thought that maybe she too was a widow or at least single. The thought crossed my mind that she might feel as lonely as I did. The last thing I wanted to do was go back to an empty house and eat alone. It wasn't that I didn't have any friends, or that I couldn't have stayed at Sherry's, or that Greg's parents and sister weren't nearby—everyone had been so wonderful. I didn't know why, but for some reason there was something else that I needed. I just longed for someone different. Because my life had become so changed.

I pushed my cart a little closer to the woman's and smiled. "Do you like these dinners?"

She smiled back and said, "Oh yes, I eat them for lunch." I was just about to ask her if she would like to come over when she frowned and said, "But my husband can't stand 'em."

The last thing I wanted to hear was the word husband. Was the whole world married? I couldn't hold back my frustration another minute. My eyes filled with tears. "I don't have a husband anymore. He died four months ago."

The poor woman looked so distressed, I immediately felt sorrier for her than myself. Of course, she wasn't expecting to get such a reaction from me. We were strangers, but still she came toward me and gave me a gentle hug. "Are you okay?" she asked.

Blushing with embarrassment, I said, "Yes. I'm so sorry."

That was the unexpected outbreak of grief that the hospice counselor had warned me about.

Sherry was finally accepted into a clinical trial at USC's Norris Cancer Center, her initial treatment scheduled for the first week of January. This gave me a renewed sense of hope for 2009. Since Sherry would be getting better, I also had to work on myself. Spending New Year's Eve alone would be a good start. If I was brave enough to spend New Year's Eve alone, that would be my turning point. I pumped myself up for the event.

After arriving home, instead of turning on both TVs, I lit candles in the bedroom, put on a Michael Buble CD, got under the covers and wrote a letter to God.

Dear God,

Today has been a good day for me. I am grateful for all I have and especially the ability to choose positive energy. This past year has held some amazing times and also the most devastating times I could ever imagine. Losing Greg has been tragic, but I will stay focused on the blessing that you gave us—we experienced the ultimate love. It was a dream come true. I know it is part of your perfect plan. I am waiting for your perfect plan to continue manifesting through me. I am here and available to be a conduit in whatever way you need me. I have no idea what this coming year holds for me, our family, our country, our earth. Thank you for allowing me this time to be with Sherry. She is my priority. I am so blessed to have such a loving daughter. I feel more hopeful with the upcoming clinical trial.

I turned the page and began a list of my goals for 2009.

Work on my old business plan. Eat healthier. Exercise. Update QuickBooks certification. Get in touch with old business contacts. My list went on and on—golf, dance, tennis, yoga, gardening, and find a new church.

I stopped writing. My list was full, but my heart was missing the most vital part of life. I wanted my husband back. I knew someday I'd have to find someone else to love. I thought about writing it down. But I didn't. I ended my list with a simple resolution: Appreciate life.

I got through New Year's and the next couple of months, but during the first two weeks of March I was angry at the world. The housing market was crashing, businesses closing up. Unemployment was on the rise. All the loss felt very personal. Sherry and I kept glued to CNN, watching the market plummet. How long would I survive on our retirement and savings? Although I did all our bookkeeping, Greg had always been the financial decision maker. I was angry at him, at the government, the banks, married people—angry even at Charlotte. Why was her career so important? Why couldn't she live down the street and have babies?

I was angry at everything and everyone—except Sherry. Sherry was right there grumbling, cussing right along with me. One afternoon, immersed in CNN, we looked at each other and grabbed for the remote. I was faster. I clicked it off. We laughed, both of us suddenly knowing that life was too precious and short to fill with anything other than happiness.

By April, I was in a much better state of mind. I'd updated my QuickBooks certification and gotten back in touch with old business contacts. Yet I knew I couldn't make any work commitments, because of Sherry's health.

One evening, out walking the dogs, I thought of specific qualities I would look for in a man someday. Kind and loving were at the top of my list. And I vowed that next time I'd be strong, more confident, and set boundaries like I should have from the beginning with Greg. I wondered if I'd ever find the courage to take my wedding ring off. That would have to be my first step.

Several days later, I called my brother-in-law Neil. Stable and steady, he was a man I held in high esteem. Neil had lost his first wife, whom he had loved very much. I had to connect with someone who understood.

At first Neil and I talked about Sherry and the weather, then I got to the point.

"I'm so lonely without Greg. Did you feel like that too

when your wife died?"

"Oh yes, very hard and difficult times," he said.

"Do you remember…taking off your ring?" I asked.

He cleared his throat. "Well…yes…I do." He paused and I felt like I had opened an old wound, but I had to know. He continued. "It was a very sad and challenging day."

"I'm sorry. This is so hard…."

"But, Rhonda, I needed to do it. That's what you need to do to move on."

I understood. I would look for the right time.

It came soon enough.

My fifty-fifth birthday was coming up soon. How much fun it was the first time Sherry and I had gone to the spa to get massages on my birthday ten years earlier, right before her graduation from dental hygiene school. She couldn't afford it, but she'd insisted on treating me. We sat in the lounge wrapped up in matching white fluffy robes and slippers, sipping lemon water, waiting to be called. We'd talked and giggled about being rich and famous someday, able to do extravagant things like this all the time. For now, we agreed on once a year for my birthday as our tradition.

Now, several days before my birthday, Sherry was at the table sipping her Vanilla Ensure. "I want to take you for your birthday massage," she said.

I didn't think it was a good idea and had no idea how she could possibly do it. For months she had been suffering from the pain of cracked ribs from coughing spells. "Do you think you can?"

Her face reddened as she drew in a breath. "I think so."
She coughed. "Yeah, I can."

My stomach churned. "Let's just wait till the last minute,
and if they just happen to have two openings, we can do it." I
didn't want to disappoint her by thinking that I wasn't
grateful for the thought, and I certainly didn't want her to get
charged for a last-minute cancellation if we didn't go.

Tuesday morning, April 21st, my birthday, I hoped
Sherry had forgotten about the massage, but she hadn't.
Despite her pain and lack of oxygen, she called a spa close to
her house. They had two appointments available and would
even give us a discounted rate since it was our first time there.

While slipping into our robes, I was more concerned
about Sherry and how she felt than anything else. Without
giving it any thought, I tucked my wedding ring into my
purse like I always did. Once on the table, I was finally able
to relax. The lavender oil, the soothing meditative music, and
being touched sent tears of gratitude leaking out the little face
rest hole. For years, Greg and I had our own massage table
and regularly gave each other massages. Towards the end of
his life, when he could only receive them, it still gave me
great comfort to touch him.

When I met Sherry back in the locker room, we
embraced. I asked her how she did. She said she was fine. By
her tone, though, I wasn't so sure. This was another reminder
that I needed to be fully in the moment with her. This could

be the last time we would have a birthday massage together.

After getting showered and dressed, I thought about my wedding ring. I could just leave it in my purse. I could put it back on if I felt the need, but for now, I'd just leave it where it was. Sherry's presence and love we shared were enough.

Ten days later, Sherry was admitted to Mission Hospital with intense pain from an erupted intestine. She was placed in the same large private room where she'd stayed when she was diagnosed two years earlier. I slept on the same couch. By now, I knew what it meant when a few stanzas of Braham's "Lullaby" played over the intercom. Another baby had been born. Whatever time of day or night it played, it always brought a smile to Sherry's and my face.

Outside Sherry's room on the second morning, I called Charlotte. I hated to tell her that her sister was in the hospital again, and that the doctors didn't believe Sherry's body could survive any more treatments. Charlotte had made so many trips back and forth from Phoenix throughout Greg's and Sherry's illnesses. I didn't want to add any stress to her hectic schedule, but she insisted on coming.

It was such a pleasure to see her, to have both my girls with me. The hardest part about being in the hospital for Sherry was that she missed her dogs so much. With Chris's approval, Charlotte and I snuck Olivia in one afternoon, hiding her in a canvas bag. We had a great time, despite the NG feeding tube in Sherry's nostril.

Six days later, Sherry was discharged. While we filled out

paperwork, Sherry's oncologist came in and suggested we talk to a hospice nurse. Sherry looked at me and shrugged. "We might as well. It was good for Dad."

Chris was at work. He and Sherry must have already talked about the possibility. I nodded.

A few minutes later, two very nice hospice nurses came in to explain all the benefits of the home health care nurses, counselors, and volunteers they would provide.

A big decision, this really meant acknowledging that Sherry would die. Sherry decided to sign up.

I decided I needed to spend every minute with her. I would rent out my townhome, fully furnished, and move in with Chris and Sherry, which meant that I had to go home and get it ready. I worked around the clock. I could've asked someone to help, but again I felt like everyone had already done so much. It wasn't easy, but I prepared the house with the determination of a marathon runner. I raced up and down the stairs, packed the attic full of personal items, took carloads to the Salvation Army. I was too tired and busy to cry. My only thought was to get back to Sherry.

Forty-eight hours later, I arrived back at Sherry's. She was happy. She sat in the corner chair of the guestroom and watched me as I unpacked my things. "I'm so happy that you'll be here all the time now," she said. I was relieved that I wouldn't have to lug all my things back and forth each week. I had been so stubborn about not wanting to be a burden to anyone, including Sherry and Chris.

Sherry giggled. "You know what?"

I turned toward her. "What?"

She tilted her head. "You're finally a stay-at-home mom."

I sat down at the end of the bed. "Wow, you're right. That's exactly what I am." My shoulders relaxed and I felt a warm tingling sensation throughout my body.

For the next three days I reveled in thinking of myself as a stay-at-home mom. I fussed and coddled over Sherry like I did when the girls were babies, but instead of trying to hurry and rush life along, I tried to make it stand still.

The following afternoon, Sherry, the dogs, and I had just settled in on the couch to watch our favorite TV game show. I looked at Sherry's feet beside me and asked, "Want a foot massage?"

She put them in my lap and said, "Sure."

I lovingly caressed her warm feet, praying I could make her healthy, again.

Then she smiled at me and said, "Mom you need to get a life."

Chapter Ten

Sherry's Bucket List

AFTER SENDING MY DATING profile into cyberspace, I was shocked to see ten matches the next morning. I'd thought the whole world was married. I skimmed the profiles, then threw on my robe. Olivia followed me downstairs. She sat on my lap while I drank a cup of coffee, waiting patiently for Sherry.

A few hours later, Sherry and I sat at the kitchen table reviewing each match. By afternoon, we were laughing like boy-crazy teens. It was a fun day, but as the time got closer for Chris to come home from work, I began to feel awkward again. *What had I done?* I knew how reserved Chris was in showing any public affection. Sherry and I were the ones always touching and hugging. He wasn't that type.

I needn't have worried. When Sherry told Chris over dinner what we had done, he wanted to see each match and gave us his opinion from a guy's perspective. I was relieved, and glad for his help.

Later that evening, I called Charlotte. I didn't bother with any chit-chat. I just started with a warning. "I've got to tell you something."

She cut me off. "Oh, Mom, I think it's great. eHarmony. Sherry and I have already talked about it. You know we text all the time." She laughed.

Despite the approval, I couldn't sleep that night. I wasn't convinced I was doing the right thing. *What would people think?* I pushed that thought aside. The only thing that mattered was having fun with Sherry. And a part of me was starting to think I might really find someone. I wondered when the next batch of matches would come in. It felt like Christmas Eve.

Every morning I woke up to eight to ten new matches. I'd skim through profiles and photos while waiting for Sherry to come downstairs. Before lunch we'd go over every detail. Some of the guys owned airplanes, boats, and wineries, and they were proud to showcase their accomplishments. There were men of all different shapes and sizes, some handsome ones and, well, some not so much. Several matches asked me to communicate with them, and at Sherry's urging, I did, but no one kept my interest, or I didn't hold theirs. I was relieved. I forgot what I had written in my own profile about wanting someone to meet Sherry. All I could think about was how I would dread it if some stranger asked me to meet him. To leave Sherry to go meet a stranger in a coffee shop was just beyond my comprehension.

One morning, I was waiting for Sherry so we could do our due diligence on each match that came in overnight. Although it had only been two weeks, it was beginning to feel like a routine. That day, however, Olivia ran through the kitchen to the doggie gate, her ears standing up, and I heard the noise I most dreaded. Violent coughing. Sherry had been coughing on and off for months, but never as she came down the stairs. I ran to the stairs and could see her doubled over at the top. I raced up, thinking she should just go back to bed.

I felt so helpless. "Oh, sweetie. What can I do?"

Sherry raised a finger, as if to say, give me a minute. Then she grabbed onto the banister, pulled herself up and continued down a few more stairs before she had to sit down again. She coughed some more. I pressed her body close to mine and held on, praying she wouldn't collapse.

My mind flooded with memories of her as a young girl when she'd wake up early and race outside to play on her swing set before breakfast and getting dressed. She always had boundless energy. In high school she was the peppiest cheerleader. In her senior year, she decided to join the gymnastic team. It didn't bother her that most of the girls had been on the team since their freshmen year; she just worked that much harder to catch up.

Now she couldn't even walk a few steps without being racked with coughing.

By the time we reached the kitchen, her coughing had ceased. Seemingly unfazed by the episode, she grabbed an Ensure out of the refrigerator, sat down at the table, and flashed a grin. "Well? Did you get any matches?"

I was still recovering from seeing her have so much difficulty coming down the stairs. But it was obvious she didn't want to dwell on that, so I went along with her.

I looked up and smiled. "Ten more."

"Awesome! Let me see!"

I showed her the ones that had come in. But after a little while, it was hard to concentrate. Something more needed to be done for Sherry. Even the portable oxygen supply hadn't made the staircase any easier for her.

Sue, the hospice nurse who came later that day, said she would order an oxygen concentrator, a machine that supplies a continuous flow of oxygen. She also told us that whenever we wanted, she could order a hospital bed for downstairs.

Sherry said, "Do it."

I was relieved her pride wasn't keeping her from being safe, but part of me still fantasized that Sherry wasn't really dying. When Chris came home from work that night, Sherry told him that an oxygen concentrator and hospital bed would be coming soon. He shrugged it off, as if he didn't believe it or hadn't even heard her. Like me, he was in denial. Then a few hours later, Sherry fell asleep on the couch. Chris covered her with a quilt and that's where she stayed all night.

Matches were still coming in nightly, but I had lost interest and had no time to read the profiles. Sherry and I had become flooded with things to do. For one thing, she had written another list.

Even when she was a young girl she was a list person. I'd get a kick out of reading the lists that she kept by her bedside in her neat handwriting: Wake up. Go to the bathroom. Get dressed. Don't forget backpack. Eat breakfast. Etc. Each task would get scratched off as she accomplished it.

This list was different. She wanted me to schedule a colonoscopy to make sure I was healthy. She wanted to host her dental hygiene class reunion for its tenth-year anniversary. She wanted to write good-bye letters.

She wanted to go through all of her things, to decide who to give what to. She wanted to give me Olivia, but she thought that would be too hard on Chris. I was disappointed, since Olivia and I had become very bonded. I told Sherry that I understood and instead she could give me back the things I had saved through the years and passed on to her when she married Chris, like her elementary awards, Student of the Day, report cards, birthday cards, old photos and letters. I made numerous trips up and down the stairs bringing her boxes so she could sort through them all. She gave me the Christmas and Halloween quilts she'd made, and wanted my sister, Joline, to finish all the other quilts she'd started.

Another diversion were the visits from the hospice staff. It seemed that once the word spread about how special Sherry was, they all wanted to visit. The nurses, spiritual counselors, social workers and volunteers all loved her because she was so full of life. Although her body was full of cancer, she didn't look or act sickly. She had a warm loving spirit with just enough straightforwardness and humor that made her real.

In elementary school, her classmates loved her, too. In fifth grade, she was picked for Student of the Day. All the kids had to write something about her.

Sherry is kind, sweet and gentle. She does her work quietly and she is my friend. But most of all I trust her. —Christine

I like you because you don't fight with anybody. You are nice. You like everybody and you care about everybody. You share a lot. I like you and I like the way you treat me. —Christy

As the end grew nearer, Sherry and I grew even closer, on a deeper level. With no separation of our energy now, like the flow between unborn baby and mother, or the never-ending love for someone who has passed on, there was a sense of urgency to grasp it, fully celebrate our bond.

Sherry and I talked about our heightened awareness clicking through this evolution of spirit like time-lapse photography of a flower opening. We talked about it, but it was difficult to explain to anyone else.

One evening, I had just given Sherry a good-night kiss

when a grave look washed over her entire being.

I held my breath and listened to the rhythmic swoosh of her oxygen.

"Mom, I don't know what my purpose in life was. Do you?"

"Sweetie, you've been the perfect daughter." I smiled, and in hopes of adding some light to her dark, then added, "Even when you were a teenager." She didn't smile back. I reminded her of what a good wife and homemaker she had been. I placed my arm around her and told her how much her dental patients loved her and how much she helped them. I reminded her how much she had done for her dogs and if she would have had the chance to become a mother, there was no doubt that she would've been the best.

But the sadness in her eyes told me I had failed to answer her question.

In my room, instead of attempting to soothe myself with my old chant—"I am at peace. God is with me"—this time I said a different prayer. I had read it many times, because the words were on one of Greg's lap-quilts, but I had never said them out loud before:

God grant me the serenity to accept the things that I cannot change, the courage to change the things I can and the wisdom to know the difference.

I slept peacefully.

The following morning, I arose to a beautiful sunrise and

began to write in my journal before I even got out of bed. After I dated the page—June 3, 2009—for some reason I titled it "Gift of Acceptance." I thought about the Serenity Prayer and accepting what I could not control. A state of being important not only for me, but for the entire universe. I wondered how I could ever accept that I had lost Greg and Sherry.

I glanced back at what I had written, thinking about Sherry and how accepting she had always been. It dawned on me then that her gift of acceptance was what Sherry came into this world to share. Whenever we talked about her death, Sherry would say she was the lucky one because she would be going to heaven. If Sherry accepted her dying, I would too.

I went downstairs with my journal, sitting and watching the morning light peep through the blinds onto Sherry's face while she slept. Before long she opened her eyes. "Good morning," she said, smiling.

I smiled and whispered, "I know what your life's purpose is."

Her eyes widened. "You do?"

I knelt down next to her. "It's to teach the gift of acceptance."

Her eyes twinkled. She stroked my hand while she waited to hear more.

I smiled. "You know—accepting the things that can't be changed?"

She nodded.

"You've always accepted everyone and everything for whom and what they are. Wouldn't it be a better world if everyone could *truly* accept the things that they can't change? Your dad had the courage to change the things that he could and you have the gift of acceptance."

She hugged me. "Mom, that's it! You've given me the best gift ever!" She sobbed tears of happiness. Rose and Olivia jumped in between us, trying to figure out if she was okay. She giggled and pushed them away from her face. "Girls, I'm better than ever—don't you worry."

I'd never seen such joy in her. I knew there was no way that something so meaningful could come from me.

I said, "Sherry, it came from God, not me. I was just the messenger." I read to her what I had written.

I could only carry on if I had Sherry's gift of acceptance with me.

That afternoon, Sherry began writing her own thoughts about what the gift of acceptance meant to her, calling it her divine purpose.

Three days later, the hospital bed arrived. A lump grew in my throat, like when Greg's was delivered ten months earlier.

When Chris arrived home from work and saw the bed in the family room, the tension between Sherry and him hit the roof. He complained that he didn't know that it was being delivered and that it made the family room look too crowded. I had never seen them have such a big argument. Of course, I wanted to defend her. *Didn't he listen when she told him it was coming!? The room wasn't that crowded.* Deep inside, I knew his complaints had more to do with his coming to terms with the fact that she was dying. He didn't want her to die, and neither did I, but I also knew the truth. She *was* dying, and I wanted her to be as safe and as comfortable as she could possibly be through the process. Chris had to accept the bed, like I had to accept it when Greg's bed had arrived. Remembering the gift of acceptance, I decided to be more accepting and gave them their space to work it out. I took the dogs for an extra walk.

It took two days for the tension to calm down to a simmer, but as soon as Sherry brought up the subject of how she envisioned her funeral service, the friction came back to a rolling boil. She said she wanted something uplifting and untraditional, like Greg's Celebration of Life had been. I thought that sounded like a great idea, but Chris disagreed. He wanted something very traditional and stiff. I thought Chris was being completely unreasonable, but I held my tongue and went to my room and wrote in my journal. *Why can't Sherry have the kind of funeral she wants?* I released my anger onto the pages, which helped me come to terms with the truth of it all. It's not the wedding that makes the marriage. It's not the funeral that depicts the soul.

The next morning, after Chris left for work, Sherry and I talked for a while. Then she casually said, "It's weird to think that I'll never go upstairs again."

My eyes narrowed and my heart ached. I felt a lump of

guilt in the center of my gut. "I'm so sorry, sweetie," I whispered. I just didn't know what else to say. I had been so caught up in being a mother and protecting my daughter that I hadn't given the consideration of the fact that upstairs was where she and Chris would never be together again.

She said we should let Chris have the funeral the way he wanted it.

I agreed.

It had been twenty-five days since I'd gotten my first ten matches, and over a week since I'd looked at any of the daily profiles. I had been awake for hours and decided to peruse the ones from that night. Greg's urn sat on the nightstand on the right side of the bed—his side. My hair was unbrushed, and I was in my pink floral nightgown. Scanning the entries, I stopped at one. The simplicity of Larry's profile caught my eye. He was wearing a black tee-shirt, Levis, and white tennis shoes, standing on the edge of the Grand Canyon Skywalk. He was tall, solid. I was attracted to his baldness and splash of gray hair above his ears. He listed his passions: family, sports, and his business. I liked that he was fifty-two, three years younger than me, healthy and active. I was touched by what he had written about the most influential person in his life: "My previous wife for teaching courage in very difficult circumstances and smiling every day." *A recent widower?* I wondered if he'd noticed that I was widowed. What would he think of what I wrote about Greg and Sherry? Would he like my smile? My blonde hair?

I heard the garage door open and close, my clue that Chris had left for work. After all the tension over the hospital bed and the funeral arrangements, I had been avoiding him. And since Sherry was sleeping downstairs in the family room, I wanted to give them their privacy in the mornings.

When I came down, Sherry was awake, sitting up in the hospital bed, looking happy. We had stored the noisy oxygen concentrator in the downstairs bedroom, so all you could see was the 50 feet of clear plastic tubing snaking down the hallway, past the bathroom, through the kitchen, over the half wall into the family room, and into Sherry's nostrils. On the hospital tray table next to her bedside were pill bottles, papers, and her laptop. Although it wasn't what I wanted to see, I noticed how much easier the bed made things for her. Her life had become more manageable having everything at her fingertips, and she was free to walk around without battling the stairs.

I gave Sherry a peck on the forehead. "Good morning, sweetie. How are you feeling?"

She swept her hand across her lap, nodded her head and smiled. "Good. This setup is so much better."

"Well," I said, "I think the dating site just got better, too." I smiled.

Sherry scooted over and patted the bed, inviting me to join her.

We logged on to my eHarmony account and read Larry's profile.

"Mom, he looks good!"

I agreed. "But what do I do now?"

"Send him a 'wink' or some questions," she said, like it was no big deal.

I ran my fingers through my hair. My pulse quickened. *Wouldn't that be considered "chasing" a man?* Greg had told me years earlier that part of his attraction to me was that I was hard to get. In the early years, when he told friends about how he had to ask me three times before I'd go out with him, he seemed so proud of that. *What would Greg think of my pursuing a stranger online? What would everyone think?*

"Maybe later," I said. If Larry was still available when I came back to the site, I'd figure out what to do then. For now, I needed to focus on getting things crossed off of Sherry's list.

Chapter Eleven

Light in Darkness

SHERRY WAS ANXIOUS TO get started on writing her good-bye letters, and she wanted them printed on nice stationary. Before I left to go shopping, Sherry tried to describe a pattern that she had in mind. I knew her tastes well enough to find something that she would be happy with, but when I arrived at the upscale, specialty stationary store it was more difficult than I'd thought.

I tried to explain to the young clerk how important it was

for me to find the perfect stationary, without telling her what it was for.

Standing in the aisle staring at the rack of paper, my mind went blank. Nothing appealed to me.

The clerk approached me again.

"It's for my daughter, not for me," I explained. "Can I return what she doesn't like?"

"I'm sorry, ma'am, but we have a no return policy," she said flatly.

I glanced down at the price and thought it was outrageous. "What if I return them in an hour?

"I'm sorry. We don't accept returns," she repeated.

My jaw tightened. I was determined. I blurted out, "My daughter's dying. She's writing her good-bye letters. She's a perfectionist, a quilter, and the pattern is important to her."

The poor girl's eyes got big, and her body froze. I began to feel sorry for her. But I stood my ground with silence.

She finally responded. "Okay. You can return anything you want."

I grabbed an armful of their rather dissatisfying colors and patterns and took them home. But Sherry didn't like any of them. I returned them all and went to Staples, around the corner, where I picked out several patterns I thought she'd like. Sherry loved them, which gave me great pleasure.

Now that Sherry had the right stationary, she settled in to write. I watched her, touched by her bravery. I wondered what and to whom she was writing, but I left her alone as she undertook these intimate final communications.

I hoped she had time enough to accomplish all she wanted. We still needed to host her dental hygiene class reunion.

The following morning, as soon as I opened my eyes, I had a very clear and powerful thought. I grabbed my journal and wrote: *I know it's crazy, but I want to write a book.* I knew it was crazy because I wasn't a *real* writer. Greg was the one who had always said he wanted to write a book, but me— never. I had played around with writing some children's poetry, and I'd written for myself, as a way to sort out my feelings during difficult times. But I now wanted to write about Greg's spiritual awakening and Sherry's gift of acceptance. That's how I could make sense out of all that had happened. These stories could help others.

I leaped out of bed and ran downstairs to tell Sherry about what I had just discovered. "Guess what I wrote?"

Her hair was going in all directions; it had lost its once smooth silky shine. "What?"

"I know it's crazy." I hesitated. "But I figured out *my* divine purpose. I'm going to write a book!" Of course, she knew exactly what I was talking about. Sherry had witnessed how kind and loving Greg had become, how our marriage had flourished. Two and a half years earlier, she'd gone with me to the women's retreat where I read the letter and shared the story about how Greg and I had found the love we'd lost. She saw how it affected the women in the group, just like the Toastmasters Club members reacted when Greg sat in the audience.

Sherry looked up at me and said, "You should!" She moved over, and I climbed into the bed beside her. I thought we would talk about the details of writing my book, but she had other things on her mind.

"Have you heard from Larry?" she asked.

I squirmed. "No," I sighed.

All of a sudden her voice got stronger. "Mom, you need to send him something!"

I was talking about my divine purpose and now she's asking me about a man with whom I hadn't even communicated yet? It was odd, because the truth was that he had been crossing my mind every hour. I would be doing the dishes and think about his photo at the Grand Canyon. I would be folding the laundry and would think about his sweet smile. Many times, I thought about the words he wrote about his wife. But there was a big difference between fantasizing about a man on an online profile and actually doing something.

I hemmed and hawed for a moment. "Well, let's look at his profile again."

Sherry grabbed her laptop from the hospital tray table and logged into my account. We scrutinized and discussed every detail.

I picked out every flaw I could find. "Why did he write 'previous' wife?"

"Well, it's obvious he meant 'late' wife," Sherry said.

Of course, I knew that's what he meant, but I had to find something to complain about.

Another part of Larry's profile we looked at was his

answer to the question, "List the things you're most thankful for."

Sherry put her fingertip on the monitor and pointed to his #1 answer: My previous 32 years of marriage.

I did the quick math. He must've been around twenty years old when he married, and be recently widowed, like me.

"He's not a player!" Sherry said. "Don't let him get away."

The harder Sherry pushed, the pickier I became. "Doesn't he look heavier in this picture than that one? I wonder if he takes care of his teeth."

"Mom, stop it!" she cried. "He's worth taking a chance. You know teeth can be fixed."

I had to laugh at myself. Sherry knew that I always cared more about character than looks. I felt that Larry had good character, but he had been alerted to my presence just the way I had been alerted to his. If he was interested in me, he would have let me know.

"I'll think about it," I said.

I knew I had some time to think about it because the following day I would be prepping for my colonoscopy. I had promised Sherry that I would have the test, and I was having it. I hoped by then Larry would have a chance to read my profile and get in touch with me. I knew that matches could go away quickly. I had seen numerous people send out notifications that they were removing their profiles because they had entered into a serious relationship.

The next two days, I was immersed in the colonoscopy

prep and procedure, but I continued to think about what Sherry had said. *What if Larry had already been taken?* The night after the test, I wrote in my journal for clarity. *Why did I feel this energy about this man, Larry?* I reminded myself again about the lessons I had learned from my marriage to Greg. Keep your wits about you! Always remain true to yourself, stay strong, and remember to set boundaries. I knew I would be okay, even if I took a risk with Larry.

The following morning I felt positive after getting a "good report" from the doctor. *Maybe Sherry was right. I do have a life ahead of me.* Life is too short to sit around and wait, and I had already spent six days doing just that. So I decided to quit waiting and at 8:45 a.m., I sent Larry five benign multiple-choice questions.

Amazingly, within a few hours he responded back with exactly the right answers.

1) Your idea of a romantic time would be:
   A) a quiet candle-lit restaurant
   B) rollerblading on the beach
   C) cooking dinner together at home
   D) getting dressed up and going to a dance club together

2) How trusting are you?
   A) sometimes I'm too naive
   B) I trust people and am able to forgive them when wronged

C) I trust people until they prove me wrong, then it is hard to trust again

D) People are dishonest by nature, you need to be careful.

3) When in a relationship, are you a jealous person?

A) I'm not the least bit jealous.

B) I don't consider myself jealous, but on occasion I have felt threatened.

C) I feel jealous every now and then.

D) I'm not overbearing or abusive, but I can be quite jealous.

4) Financially, how would you characterize yourself?

A) Very frugal and financially conservative.

B) Good at saving money with occasional unplanned purchases.

C) Adventuresome with investments and spending.

D) I'm responsible, but I believe in spending money to enjoy life, without too much worry about tomorrow.

5) Do you consider yourself physically affectionate when involved in a relationship?

A) Sure, I love to hold hands, hug and give casual kisses.

B) I'm moderately affectionate. I like to hold hands and exchange hugs.

C) I do like a small amount of physical affection.

D) I don't consider myself a very physically affectionate person.

I loved all his answers. They were exactly the ones I was looking for. When I showed Larry's answers to Sherry, she had *I told you so* written all over her face. I couldn't wait to find out more about him. The next step of the guided communication was to pick out the ten most important things listed on the "*must haves*" in a relationship. Of course, I wanted to have all forty things listed, but the website only allowed me to pick ten, which made me really think about what was the most important. It wasn't easy. Was it more important to have my partner be spiritual, loyal, responsible, affectionate, kind, and patient or emotionally healthy, reserved, and traditional in their sexual needs? Then, it worked the same for the "can't stands." Was poor hygiene, pessimism, denial, and arrogance more significant to me than lying, addiction, laziness, and mean spiritness? I sent him my list of "Must Have's and "Can't Stands" and requested his. We weren't dead on with all of our choices, but we were on the same page.

Chapter Twelve

Larry

MORE BUTTERFLIES BUILT UP in my stomach each time I reread what Larry wrote. He seemed like the perfect man. The first three things I wanted to know were about his children, his business, and his interests. These were all set questions in the "guided communication" part of the website, so I didn't even have to think too hard.

Hi Larry, How many children do you have and can you

tell me about them?

I have 2 daughters.

I thought how perfect, just like me.

The older (Lisa, age 26) has been married for almost 3 years to a really great guy. We found out about a month ago that Lisa is pregnant and due on my birthday in December.

My motherly mind immediately went into high gear. *How was Lisa feeling?* Pregnancy hormones, alone, can wreak havoc, but grieving for your mother on top of it was unfathomable. I remembered how horrible I felt after my mother died. Although I didn't think I had the best mother in the world, it felt like I had a giant gaping hole in my heart when she was gone. Like a teenager who starts thinking about taking the last name of her latest crush, I had already begun to think how I could help Lisa and how she in return could help me. A sweet little baby coming into the world was such a blessing!

My younger daughter (Gina, age 22) recently married a guy who is in the Navy and stationed in Florida.

What strong girls his daughters must be, to be continuing on with their lives despite their great loss. Their parents must have taught and prepared them well.

What type of business do you have and do you love your work?

With a business partner, I own a company that does mostly kitchen and bath remodeling. We've been in business for about 8 years and have done fairly well at it. The economy has caused ups and downs, but we've seen things getting better lately. I love parts of the business and I dislike other parts. I've been doing a lot of soul searching lately (since my wife died) concerning all aspects of my life and making sure I go forward with what I want and leave behind what I don't want. I've come to the conclusion that I'm really happy with just about everything, except losing my best friend of 32 years. I've also realized I can't change that, so I just go forward without her. So, in answer to your question, I mostly love my work.

Wow! I thought what an honest man who is capable of expressing himself freely without being sappy or complaining. He even has the gift of acceptance.

Describe an interest you have that you would truly hope your partner could share with you.

This is a hard one. I spent most of my free time in the past 8 years taking care of my wife while she was ill and working to develop our business. We did quite a bit of traveling and I really like that. I'd hope my new partner would have an interest in "seeing the world."

I knew how difficult it was to be a caregiver, and I had only been doing it for 2 ½ years. My heart went out to him. *Eight years?* That meant taking care of his wife while raising teenage girls. I wasn't embarrassed to write back and tell him I cried while reading his answer.

I felt he could well be the kind and loving man that I had been praying for. Although I didn't like all the packing and prep that went into travel, I thought this man so deserved to "see the world" with a healthy woman.

The next morning Larry wrote:

I'm sorry for bringing you tears, but I understand. Thank you for expressing sorrow about my wife. I'm sorry for the loss of your husband, and I can't imagine what you must be going through with your daughter.

I'd also like to keep the communication open. I'm sure at the very least we understand each other's position in life, somewhat. I'm always hearing people compare the loss of my wife to losing their parents, but my father died 2 years ago and while it was difficult, it doesn't even come close to losing my wife.

I'm very new to online dating, as a matter of fact, I haven't even thought of dating in any form for over 30 years. I found my wife when I was 20 years old and never spent any time after that looking around. As I'm not well versed in online dating etiquette,

I apologize in advance for my mistakes.

I should tell you that we'll have plenty of time to communicate over the internet before even considering meeting because I'm on a long vacation. I wasn't able to take much time off when my wife died in March because we were relocating our business. On May 31st, I drove away from North County headed towards Canada. About 1 week later, I made it to Vancouver and turned right. Last Thursday, I was in Portland, Maine and turned right again. At the present time I'm headed down the East Coast and I'm in New Jersey. In about a week, I'm meeting my younger daughter, Gina, in Florida, where her husband is stationed. I'll make another right turn from there and head towards New Mexico, and then I'll drive up to Wyoming and then back to San Diego. I'm about half way through my trip now, so I'm planning on being back in North County sometime around the end of July. I took this time off to reevaluate everything in my life, as I said earlier. I really would like to hear more about your family, and I see you're retired and starting a new business. Please tell me more.

Thanks for sharing.

Larry

My heart pounded. Larry not only seemed like the perfect man; now I was convinced he was, since he wasn't available to meet me anytime soon. When all this started, I couldn't imagine leaving Sherry to go out on a date. Besides, writing and answering questions felt so much safer. It made me think back to fifth grade, when everyone in my class had to write a pen pal in another state. I did it myself once or twice, but it never worked out for me. Yet I heard there were people who wrote to their pen pals for decades. So I thought of Larry as my pen pal, a friend who understood.

Feeling safe about Larry, I opened up and told him more about my life, and he did the same.

That afternoon Larry wrote:

Rhonda, Thanks for giving me so much information about yourself. It sounds like you've had an interesting, tough, and wonderful life so far. I admire your courage for hanging in there when things were not so good and your ability to go another direction when you realized things weren't going the right direction. I'm sorry to hear Sherry is apparently very close to the end of her life. It never makes sense when someone so young is facing that, but I know we don't make those plans, we just live them. Maybe someday we'll understand that Grand Plan.

I watched similar circumstances unfold with my wife, Rosemary. We lived a very "normal" life from the time we met in 1977 until 2001. A few days after 9/11, Rosemary was diagnosed with Lymphangioleiomyomatosis (LAM). Briefly, LAM is caused by a genetic defect and causes smooth muscle cells to grow on the inside of your lungs, along with several other symptoms. The lungs are not able to absorb oxygen like normal lungs, so she was on oxygen for about two years. After a visit to National Institute of Health in Bethesda, MD, a recommendation was made to investigate a lung transplant since that was the only treatment for the disease. We went through the evaluation, listing for transplant, and then waiting to make the "Top of the List." Finally, in July 2003, she received a double lung transplant. No more oxygen and things were a lot better for about 3 years. Then, she started developing rejection of the lungs. It caused small issues and then larger ones. Towards the end, she went back on oxygen, and at the very end, even that wasn't enough. There were a lot of other health issues including 2 different types of cancer, but I'll save those for another time. Rosemary also died very peacefully, she knew she'd done her job and it was time to move on. I watched Rosemary go through all of those problems, and I have to say she never had a bad day during any of it. She was the most positive person I've ever met! I miss her greatly, but I also recognize I need to move on and enjoy the next 30 years of my life. Our relationship was as close to perfect as you can get. We were both very skilled at "Giving more than you receive," because we realized by doing so, you'd still get more out of the relationship than you put in. We brought our two wonderful daughters into the world and watched them mature into positive, productive adults who hopefully will enjoy the same kind of environment that they were brought up in.

It seems like we've taken two different paths to end up in very similar circumstances. I look forward to growing our friendship and who knows...

If there is anything I can do for you, please let me know. There isn't much I can do from the East Coast, but I'm happy to be someone you can talk to who's been through similar things.

Thanks for taking time to listen to my story. I hope things go as well as possible for Sherry. And, as a caregiver, you know you

have to take care of yourself first, so you can take care of her.
Sincerely
Larry

I was touched, again, by Larry's response. I liked the way he described his relationship with his late wife and how he understood that when both partners *give* they both *receive* more in the end. It reminded me of the adage—the sum of all the parts is greater than the whole. I thought how true that became for Greg and me. A part of me ached that Greg and I hadn't figured things out sooner, but I was still grateful that we did before it was too late. But now that I was older, I didn't have the time or energy to go through all that again. I had to get it right from the start this time.

So far, Larry had my approval, and each time I shared his responses with Sherry, she agreed. Yet still, I felt like I needed more support and insight from others.

I called my three older sisters and my dear friend Shelley to tell them about Larry. They all seemed to approve and were happy for me, but that didn't surprise me. I was like a kid going to the one parent who was more likely to give her what she wanted.

Even though I had gotten the initial positive response from Charlotte after I had first signed up on eHarmony, I wanted to tell her what I was specifically learning about Larry and how I was feeling about him. When it came to dating, Charlotte had always been cautious and analytical, but that didn't mean that I couldn't read her emotions. I would know what she was thinking, and if she had any strong opinions about Larry, she would let me know. I called and told her what had happened—that I had made this connection, and that I was pursuing whatever it was that Larry and I had. A long-distance romance? A special pen pal relationship? Charlotte truly sounded happy for me—and so I kept writing Larry, looking forward each day to what he would send me, and to the times when I could write him back.

After six days of "guided communication," I needed more. I had to hear Larry's voice. *Was this man for real?* After taking Rose and Olivia out for a walk, I scrolled down the list on my cell phone contacts, heart pounding, and stopped on LARRY. I had programmed it on my phone as soon as he emailed it. I wanted to call him right then, but I couldn't get up the nerve, even though he had said to call anytime. *What would people think?*

Finally, I hit "send" and held my breath.

One ring. "This is Larry."

"Hi, Larry. This is Rhonda."

"I'm so glad you called." His voice was so calm. I immediately relaxed. I figured I'd eventually feel that way, but didn't think it would happen so fast. It felt like he was my long-lost friend. It was heaven to hear the inflections in his voice, to feel his tempo. To be honest, I mainly talked about Greg and about how much I missed him. Larry mainly talked about Rosemary and how much he missed her. There was no need to apologize for how either of us felt; it was so natural and good to get it all out in the open. I had read in the widow dating advice that it wasn't a good idea to talk about the dead spouse to the new date. *Who made up that rule?* To me, the important thing was to be honest. Of course, I knew we had many other things to talk about, and we would, but after an hour I needed to get back to Sherry.

When I walked into the family room, Chris was sitting with Sherry in her hospital bed. It made me feel that much happier to see them together enjoying each other's company. They were laughing about how comfortable it was to have a bed with a remote control in the family room. The thought that love begets love crossed my mind. Ever since I had started communicating with Larry, things were so much better between Chris and Sherry.

Then all of a sudden Sherry looked at my face. "Wow, Mom, you've got it bad."

I blushed. "I just talked to Larry," I said.

Rose and Olivia jumped up on the bed. I sank into the couch and filled Sherry and Chris in on all the details.

Then I kissed Sherry good-night, smiled at Chris, and floated up the stairs to my room.

I continued having daily phone conversations with Larry. We talked while I walked the dogs, after I went to bed, and in the early mornings before Sherry awakened. All the while, Larry continued driving down the East Coast and into the Florida Panhandle, checking in and out of hotels, and eating in restaurants alone.

We soon learned that our houses were only five miles apart. I knew of his neighborhood, and he knew all about mine. We laughed about how ironic it was that we lived in similar retirement golfing communities and yet neither of us were at home enjoying the benefits. I was in Orange County taking care of Sherry, and he was driving down the East Coast trying to figure out what to do with his life. Larry suggested that we pick a specific topic of discussion for what we would talk about next time. We weren't getting any younger. We had to be honest with each other, so we stayed focused. We talked about religion, our health, values, morals, food choices, lifestyles, and finances. Both of us kept saying how amazed we were of how much we aligned with each other. Although we were done raising our children, we still talked about what values we thought were most important to impart on our children while they were young. We even talked about when they were teenagers and whether or not we bought them their first cars. It was an interesting and worthwhile conversation because it was another indication of how much we were on the same wavelength. We talked about how much we loved our daughters. In one conversation, I bluntly told Larry what a good catch I was, and he immediately responded, "I know you are. And so am I." I loved his answer.

While I was acting like a teenager talking on the phone for hours, Sherry and Chris were acting like lovebirds. I had never seen Chris so relaxed and affectionate. One night over dinner Chris smiled and filled his plate with meatloaf and mashed potatoes while Sherry reminisced about how their romance started. Chris was one of Sherry's dental instructors during hygiene school. Several weeks before graduation a buzz started going around campus of what a perfect match Sherry and Chris would be. Chris was shy, sweet and very handsome. The day after graduation, he asked her out. I had heard the story many times before, but it was so refreshing to see them reliving the memories. And now here they were, helping each other through one of life's biggest transitions, being as vulnerable as two people can be with each other, facing the worst thing that can befall a couple.

A big moment in my own romance with Larry came late Saturday night. I was propped up on a pile of bed pillows talking to Larry on the phone in my room.

He said, "I've been thinking about what you wrote in your profile."

He sounded so serious. "What?" I couldn't imagine what he was talking about. We'd already talked about every possible topic.

"About you wanting someone to meet Sherry," he said.

At first my memory came flooding back to that calm and peaceful feeling I had before I wrote the words: *My daughter has terminal cancer and she is my life right now. Why would I be on a dating site? She's encouraging me to move on with my life. What a treat it would be if you had the opportunity to meet her. She is an angel.*

Then I remembered how, after I had read it aloud to

Sherry, she said, "Perfect, Mom, perfect." It was so crystal-clear at the time, yet I hadn't given it another thought since. But Larry was right. That's exactly what I had wanted. I couldn't deny it.

But that's not what I wanted right now. All I wanted now was for everything to stay exactly the way it was. I wanted Sherry and Chris to stay happy and loving towards each other. I wanted to stay safe and secure in a long-distance relationship. I said nothing.

Larry sighed. "Well, that very first day when I read your profile, I honestly thought you had written those words directly to me."

At first I thought his comment sounded a little cheesy. *How could he think I wrote that for him? Why didn't he send me the first communication, then?*

Larry went on with his story. "I set out on this long road trip to figure out what I wanted in my life, and by the time I reached Oregon, I realized that I needed a life partner. That night after I checked into the Crater Lake Lodge, I signed up for eHarmony, but it was more out of curiosity than anything else. I wondered if there were there any single women out there who would be right for me. I wondered how these dating sites work. I figured by the time I got home from my trip I'd be ready to start communicating with someone. Six days later, I was in a little roadside motel in Portland, Maine, when I first read your profile. You caught my eye. You lived close by, you were attractive, widowed, and seemingly intelligent. But honestly, Rhonda, my biggest problem came when I came to the end and read what you wrote about Sherry. I felt overwhelmed. I didn't know if I was up to the task of dealing with more death and dying."

I knew exactly what he was talking about. "Yes," I whispered into the phone. Tears rolled down my cheeks.

He said, "But now that we've gotten to know each other, even if nothing else develops, we'll always be friends." Larry cleared his throat and continued. "I had to say something, you know, I'd regret it the rest of my life if Sherry died before I had the chance to meet her. I don't want her to be a legend."

I nodded. I understood. He didn't want to just hear the stories about her, and besides, it was my request.

Larry said, "A week from tonight I'll be in Texas for my family reunion. I was thinking after that I could leave my car at my mother's and fly home for a couple of days to meet you and Sherry."

I was surprised and touched by the fact that he had given it so much thought, but I liked it the way it was between us— a romance from afar, a fantasy man come to life, but not *wholly* to life.

I couldn't give him an answer. I took a deep breath. "Well, I'll think about it, but it's getting late so I better go," I said, "Sherry's hygiene group reunion party is tomorrow."

Larry said, "I promised myself I wouldn't say it yet but...I love you."

My shoulders relaxed. I was feeling the same way about him. Even so, I couldn't say it. I just couldn't. "Thank you," I said instead.

All night, Larry's words ran through my head. He could fly home for a couple of days to meet me and Sherry. He felt like my words had been directly written to him. What if he never had the chance to meet Sherry? He loved me. I had obviously put a request out for the whole world to see. How could I renege on it? Then I wondered if Larry sensed that Sherry was closer to death than any of us realized. I buried my head under the pillow. I didn't want to think about Sherry dying. But I knew I needed to give Larry some kind of answer. I just didn't know what it would be. For now, I needed to take care of Sherry.

I was up bright and early the next morning to get ready for the brunch. Each of Sherry's classmates would bring a dish to share, but I still had a few old favorite recipes I wanted to make. Since I had begun communicating with Larry, the mood in the house had changed so drastically that it seemed like we were having a party every day. Although, for right now, I was glad I had something specific to focus on instead of Larry's question.

Sherry showered while I made up her hospital bed with the pink sheets and floral comforter she had bought online. It made the bed blend into the room so well, it was hardly noticeable. When she came out of the bathroom, I was impressed by her beauty and stamina. She was able to apply her make-up and blow dry her hair without my help.

Everything set and ready for the guests to arrive, Sherry and I sat down on the couch to rest.

"Well, I have a problem," I said.

Sherry's brow furrowed. "What?"

"Last night, Larry asked if he could fly out to meet us."

"When?" she asked.

"In about a week, or so, I guess. After his family's reunion."

Sherry gave me a confused look, as if to say, Are you *asking* or *telling?* I clarified myself, "I didn't give him an answer. I don't know...."

"Mom, you should have him come. I mean, after all, you don't want to waste any more time with him if there's no chemistry."

I sniffed the air and jumped up off the couch. "I better check the casserole."

Chemistry? I never expected her to say that. *Don't waste any more time?*

What I thought she'd say was that having Larry fly back to meet us in person was a ridiculous idea because we didn't really know him. Sure, he seemed nice enough in writing and on the phone, but what if he was some kind of weirdo? We had Googled him, checked out his business website, read the local newspaper story about Rosemary's double lung transplant. The article specifically said that it took a strong supportive family for any patient to go through such a procedure and talked highly about Larry and his daughters. But this wasn't the time to make any mistakes or take any precious time away from Sherry.

Laughter, tears, and conversation filled Sherry's family room as I busied myself in the kitchen, refilling the girls' mimosas and offering them finger foods. Debi, a side-line professional photographer, brought her camera and took individual and group shots. Sherry picked up the framed photo that was taken on Christmas night two days after she had turned nine. In it, she was thanking me with a hug and a kiss for a surprise birthday gift that I had purposely held back so I could surprise her one more time.

"Hey, let's reenact this picture," Sherry said.

We both did our best to get in the same exact position, but it was a little awkward with her oxygen cannula. All the girls watched and coached us on how and where to place our hands, arms, and lips.

After the photo was snapped, Sherry made the announcement. "My mom's in love. His name's Larry." I didn't know if the subject would come up. I felt the blood rush into my cheeks as everyone turned towards me. *Why was I falling in love at such an inopportune time?*

I started out with the disclaimer. "Well, it's only been ten days, I haven't actually even met him...yet." The girls wanted all the details, like girls do. So I started from the beginning, about how Sherry wanted me to "get a life."

By mid-afternoon, after Sherry's classmates had said their good-byes, I cleaned up the kitchen, feeling so good to have shared my news. Then I joined Sherry, who was now reclined in bed. She stroked my arm. "You know what was so ironic about today?"

"What?"

"Here I'm the one dying, and you and I were the two happiest people at the party." She smiled.

I closed my eyes. She was right. We were celebrating. Then I thought about Larry. He deserved an answer. I would ask Chris what he thought. He'd never approve of inviting some strange man into his house.

Chapter Thirteen

I Am Woman

LATER THAT NIGHT, I called Larry to fill him in about the party. I told him how much fun the reenactment photo shoot was and how Debi would do her best to photoshop out the oxygen tubes. Larry told me how much he'd enjoyed spending time with his younger daughter, Gina, and her new husband in Florida. We talked for several hours. Then there was a pregnant pause.

My heart beat faster.

I prayed he wouldn't ask me again about flying out to meet us. I was still unsure. But I thought about what Sherry said about chemistry, and of course she was right: How could I ever know if Larry was the right one without meeting him in person? How had I gotten myself into this mess?

Larry sighed. "Well, I know you've had a long day. Say 'hi' to Sherry for me and get some good rest."

Feeling relieved, I held my breath for a brief moment. I closed my eyes. "Okay, I will. Good night. I'll call tomorrow."

I sank my head into the pillows, trying to drown out my thoughts. I envisioned what it would be like to have Larry sitting downstairs visiting with Sherry and me. I could see the three of us laughing and enjoying each other's company the way Greg, Sherry, and I did when we'd sit around and talk about dentistry. I could see Larry playing a game of backgammon with Sherry while I watched, like I did when she played with Greg. I wanted Larry to experience her warm and loving spirit. I knew he'd love her, because everyone did. I suppose I was also trying to recreate the family that I was losing.

Then my mind drifted, thinking about the Prince Charming that Sherry often spoke about whenever she mentioned Disneyland or Chris. It had always sounded so corny and childish to me that she thought so romantically. Of course these things don't happen in real life. I wondered what it would be like to feel Larry's arms around me, to feel his lips on mine. I wondered if there would be chemistry.

Unable to sleep, I also thought about when the right time

would be to tell Greg's parents, sister, and brother. Through the years, we had traveled and spent every birthday and holiday together. Shouldn't they know what I was doing? Would they judge me? I thought back to the day of Greg's funeral, when one of his old patients came up to me in the parking lot before the service started and handed me his phone number and said to call him if I needed to talk. It put me on guard. *So inappropriate*, I thought at the time. Even Greg's sister, Bev, agreed with me when I told her about it. A few months later, when I was in the height of my own grief, I felt bad for being so critical of Greg's patient. I knew that his longtime girlfriend had died of cancer the year before and realized he was probably trying to reach out to someone who he thought could understand. Rather than risk that kind of misjudgment, I thought it was easier not to think about breaking the news to any of Greg's family. Besides, Larry and I hadn't even met yet.

I finally drifted off to sleep after telling myself that everything would be solved in the morning when Chris told Sherry and me that we were crazy for even thinking about inviting Larry to visit.

In the morning, I asked Chris, and he shocked me by saying, "Sure, have him come."

But I still wasn't convinced. Sue, the hospice nurse, had made it very clear that this was Sherry's time to spend with whomever she wanted, and I agreed. So I asked Sherry several more times that day if she was sure about Larry coming. Her answer remained the same—and so did all my confusion.

By late afternoon, I thought all my problems had been solved. Sherry's health seemed to be getting better and better. I mean, after all, Sherry was able to get herself all dolled up for the reunion the day before. Of course, she was still connected to the oxygen, but she was able to enjoy her party like everyone else. She hadn't had any recent coughing spells and seemed to be pain free. I thought since she was getting so much better, there wouldn't be any reason for Larry to fly back. He would be back home in a month, anyway. In fact, I was so grateful how well Sherry was doing that I composed a group email to let all of our friends and family know how hopeful I remained and how grateful I was to be her "stay-at-home mom." Of course, I wanted to tell them all about Larry, but it just wasn't the appropriate time.

Later that evening, while I walked the dogs, I decided not to call Larry. I just needed time to mull things over.

After I retreated into my room for the night, I longed to hear Larry's voice. It was late, but I couldn't resist. It felt like forever since we had last talked, even though it had been less than 24 hours. He was happy to hear from me, and we talked for several hours. I wanted to give him an answer, but the words just wouldn't come out of my mouth. When we said our good-nights, I was so relieved he didn't bring it up.

All night, I lay there, resting but not sleeping, as if I were immersed in a warm, calming bath. I felt no pressure, and because of that, clarity emerged.

Tuesday morning as the sun came up over the horizon, I knew without a doubt that Larry was the right man for me. I sent him an email.

Larry,

I haven't slept all night. I can't stop thinking about you and I think it is because you're sweeter than sweet. You better make those flight reservations. Now, maybe I can get some sleep.

Love,

Rhonda

That afternoon, Larry called and said he had made his reservations. He'd fly into San Diego late Monday night, I could meet him on Tuesday, and if everything went well he would come up and meet Sherry on Wednesday. And he would love it, if there was time, if I could meet his daughter Lisa and her husband. Tuesday and Wednesday were perfect, since those were Chris's days off. It all sounded like a good plan until Larry asked me where I'd like to meet him.

This threw me into to a tizzy. Reality hit. I wiped the perspiration off my brow and told him I'd have to think about it. *Thank god I have a week to decide.*

For three days, I did my best to avoid thinking about any details of our upcoming meeting. I kept reminding myself that I had plenty of time, but by Friday morning it felt like a bomb was ticking in my hip pocket. I needed to come up with a plan. But what if someone thought of me as a loose woman, a bad mother, or an inappropriate widow? I didn't think I could stand it.

I had to talk to Sherry, but she was still asleep. I tiptoed into the family room, where Rose and Olivia were curled up at her side. I sat in the same Queen Anne chair where I had sat while Sherry had taken my dating profile photos almost seven weeks earlier. I watched Sherry's chest rise and fall as I played out possible scenarios of where I could meet Larry. First, I thought of a restaurant, but the more I thought about it, the less I liked the idea. I figured that one way or another, I'd be a bumbling idiot. I had no idea what kind of emotions I'd face, but I was certain they'd be there. *Would I sob because Larry wasn't Greg? Would I cry tears of happiness because there was chemistry between us, or would I cry if there wasn't? Would I regret this years later, having wasted precious time away from Sherry?* No matter how I turned it upside down or inside out, I was certain to be a mess, so I ruled out a restaurant. I wanted to spare us both the embarrassment.

I rubbed my eyes. I had to come up with a different plan. I thought, since I'd spent so many hours talking to Larry while I walked, maybe that could be an option. Numerous times, Larry had told me how much he enjoyed walking and that it was the one thing he wished Rosemary could've done with him, but she was just too sick. I thought about how romantic it would be to walk, hand in hand, at the beach. But what if it wasn't? What if I cried and ran out of tissues? Was

I just making up excuses, setting myself up for disaster?

Sherry stirred, then with no effort at all, she sat up. She said, "Never what if. Always thank God."

I stood up. "What did you say?" I had heard her, yet I didn't understand what she meant.

In order to make her point clear, she repeated herself, this time speaking louder and slower.

I still wasn't sure what she meant, but it was obviously very important to her. Instead of asking her to explain herself, I handed her a piece of note paper and told her to write it down.

In her clear handwriting she wrote:

It's Never—what if?
It's Always—thank God.
Moms are ordinary people
Doing extraordinary things

She smiled and handed it to me. "Here you go."

I folded it up and put it in my pocket. I figured that we could talk about it later, but for now I needed her advice. "I've been sitting here trying to figure out where to meet Larry on Tuesday."

"How about Starbucks?"

I crinkled my nose and shook my head. "That would be too weird."

Sherry coughed. "Well, you have to meet in public."

In my mind, I'd already nixed a restaurant and a walk on

the beach. Of course, meeting at the movies wouldn't work. What would be the point? I wanted to sit with him, read his face, and gaze into his eyes. I wanted to be absolutely certain that he was the right man for me—the man worthy of meeting Sherry.

I turned my head and stared out the window. "Well, who's to say that a public place is the only safe place?" I began to think about the possibility of meeting at his house.

On Sunday morning, my friend Shelley drove up to Sherry's. The three of us discussed where I should meet Larry. I appreciated that they cared so much for my safety. They were insistent that I should meet him in a public place.

I smiled and nodded. Of course, I understood what they were saying, but I didn't agree.

"But...this is different." I knew what I was doing. I'd spent a lifetime learning how to get it right. I was positive that I didn't want to meet Larry in public. I totally trusted him. I needed my privacy.

But they both ignored me. They huddled over the computer, scouring his Facebook page for clues. They reread the newspaper article about his wife having the double lung transplant. It was hilarious; they were worse than two mother hens.

After another hour of pleading, they finally agreed, with the stipulation that I would call and text them throughout the day. They made it clear that they would be checking in with each other, too. The three of us agreed that, if needed, I would spend Tuesday night at Shelley's, since she just lived ten minutes from Larry's, and Sherry was a full hour away.

I stood up and curtsied. "Thank you."

Now, all I needed to do was to tell Larry my plan.

That same evening, Rose and Olivia pulled on their leashes in opposite directions while I fumbled with my cell phone.

"Hi Larry, I've been thinking about where to meet. I want privacy."

"I get it, believe me, I understand," he said.

"How about your house?"

"Do you really think that's a good idea?"

"I do. If my house wasn't rented, we could meet at mine."

"Well, I'd love to meet at mine, but on the surface it sounds like a bad idea. Of course, I know it'll be alright because I know myself. You'll be safe."

I laughed and nodded. "That's very kind of you."

"I won't tell you no, but don't ever do this again." I knew what he meant. He wanted to protect me, but I had already learned how to protect myself. I appreciated his advice and took it as thoughtful and caring, not patronizing.

After we hung up, I patted myself on the back. I had listened to others' opinions, but I recognized what I needed. I had held firm in being true to myself. I was excited.

Chapter Fourteen

Chemistry

EARLY TUESDAY MORNING, I spent extra time showering, blow drying, applying make-up, and dressing. I packed a small overnight bag. I didn't know for sure if I'd be needing it or not. I had no idea if I'd spend all day with Larry or an hour; I'd have to see how it went. I didn't like driving the freeways at night, and if it got dark, I was prepared to go spend the night at Shelley's.

When I came downstairs, I thought I'd find Sherry

asleep. I'd give her a gentle kiss good-bye and slip out the front door. But she was bright-eyed and cheerful. She looked like she had been awake for hours.

I glanced down at my watch: 7:30 a.m. It would take at least an hour or more, depending on the traffic. I had a few minutes to spare. I was doing my best to keep my cool. "Let's double check," I said, "Make sure you have Larry's phone number and address." We had already checked all those details during Shelley's visit on Sunday, but I wanted to be sure.

Everything was good to go.

I stood up and lingered by Sherry's bedside. Was I being reckless? On the outside, I knew it could appear that way to others, and that concerned me. Yet, on the inside, I knew differently. I reminded myself that it just happened to be that nothing was the way it was supposed to be. Greg wasn't supposed to be dead. Sherry wasn't supposed to be dying. I wasn't supposed to be traipsing off to meet some strange man.

But Larry didn't feel like a stranger; he felt like my best friend. I couldn't wait to meet him. I had made a commitment to Sherry, and now I had made one to Larry. No matter the consequences that lay ahead of me, no matter what anyone would think, it was time to follow through.

"Well, I better leave now."

Right before I turned to leave, Sherry said, "I've written some instructions for you." She handed me a note from her tray-side.

I read it and sighed with relief.

Have a great time. Be safe, be happy. <u>No guilt!</u> Love, Sherry the Girls & Chris
P.S. Bring up the issue that you're a <u>nervous</u> passenger <u>in the car!</u>

It was exactly what I needed—that final push of permission to move on with my life, safely, happily, and guilt free. I gave her a kiss on the cheek, leaving a smudge of my lipstick, and turned to leave.

She said, "Oh, I forgot…. One more thing."

I turned around and raised my eyebrows. "Yes?"

She smiled and said, "Ask him who has control of the TV remote."

I chuckled, then picking up the pen on her tray, I wrote: Control over the TV remote? "Now, I won't forget." I winked.

Driving south on I-5, I was no longer the grieving widow. I was a woman on a mission to start her new life. I thought about the Serenity Prayer. It wasn't only about accepting the things we cannot change. It was also about having the courage to change the things that we can. Sherry and Greg had been instrumental in guiding me toward that light of courage, but soon I would have to do it all on my own.

Larry's slow steady voice came from my cell phone

speaker. "You're getting closer. I can see your car now."

"Fifth house on the left. Right?" I said, for at least the tenth time.

Then I saw him standing there waving me into his driveway and holding a single long-stemmed white rose.

Before I knew it, my body leaned into his as I gazed into his blue eyes. His eyes took me to a place of no return; there was *lots* of chemistry. We embraced in front of his house for all the neighbors to see. He gently pulled me a little closer and kissed me. His lips were soft and full. While our lips touched in a tender kiss, I imagined that we looked like two lovers who'd been separated for years. Larry's body was strong and solid. His touch was gentle and fluid. I felt life.

We pulled away for a moment, our eyes locked again. We were double checking to make sure we hadn't lost our minds. I reached up and touched his bald spot. Then we laughed. It was for real—we both knew it.

"I thought I'd feel sad, but you know, I feel great." Then he paused for a moment and looked into my eyes and said, "I could spend the rest of my life with you."

"Me, too!" I shook my head in disbelief. I never imagined that it would be so relaxed, so easy.

Once inside, I immediately spotted a picture of Rosemary sitting on a ledge in the entryway. I picked it up. "When was this taken?"

"A few years ago," Larry answered.

I held my eyes steady on the photo, hoping to connect with Rosemary. She was sitting on Santa's lap with a big smile on her face. I thought, *How fun*. That was something I could picture myself doing if I ever had the chance. With closer inspection, I could see that she was a gentle, good woman. I could see it in her eyes. I went deep into my quiet space of reverence to let her know how much I respected her, her home, and her husband. I waited. Before I knew it I felt like she had not only welcomed me in, but that she had been part of the bigger plan.

There was a comfortable great room open to the kitchen with large windows along the length of an entire wall. Attracted to the view, I walked toward the windows. Outside was a large greenbelt area with hills in the background, and to the right Lake San Marcos. It was beautiful.

Larry stood beside me, but I could tell that he was anxious for me to notice something else. He pointed behind us to the vase filled with white roses sitting on the kitchen's island. "It wasn't easy to find those at seven this morning."

I walked over and buried my nose in delight. "They're gorgeous!" I had never seen such stunning roses.

"I went to two different floral stands. They had to be perfect and white."

I appreciated his candor and resourcefulness. I knew his flight had come in at ten the night before. I was touched that he had remembered a passing comment I made during one of our conversations that white flowers were my favorite.

As I looked around, it was obvious that Rosemary and I had different tastes in décor. She picked Southwestern prints, dream catchers and wolves, whereas I prefer, lace, white flowers and all shades of green.

"Rosemary loved all her things, but like I've told you, I'm okay with just about anything," Larry said. I appreciated how intuitive he was, because my surroundings are very important to my well-being. I knew that if we were to move forward, all these details would need to be worked out. I had heard the horror stories about widowers who expected to keep everything the way their late spouse had left them. I knew that would never work for me.

Within a few minutes after settling onto the couch with Larry, I got my first text from Sherry: *Did you show him the note?*

I laughed. I had.

Larry said, "Let her know that I'll promise to drive safely and the remote will always be yours!"

So I texted her back: *All is good here, sweetie. He's wonderful! Love, Mom*

Larry and I talked in between the barrage of phone calls and text messages. My sisters called to check up on me to see how it was going. Charlotte, Sherry, and Shelley were texting each other. In the meantime, Larry was fielding his own text messages and calls from his daughters.

At noon, Larry suggested that we go for a walk to get lunch. "LeAnn's Café isn't too far away."

We held hands as we walked through his neighborhood to the local café. We were offered a booth right away. We sat on the same side and giggled like teenagers. It felt so good to laugh.

I nuzzled in closer to him and whispered, "Can you believe this?"

Larry pulled me in a little tighter. "If the people in here knew the whole story they'd be blown away."

We laughed. *What was so funny?* Here I thought I'd be bawling my eyes out. Now I had never felt so free to be myself. My cheeks ached from smiling and laughing so much that I could hardly eat my half of the sandwich we shared.

After we got back to the house, I made a thousand trips to the bathroom. Either I was getting a UTI or something else was happening. I kept drinking glass after glass of water, hoping it would help, but it didn't. Larry kept asking me if I was alright, and I kept saying yes. Before we knew it, twelve hours had flown by and it was time for me to leave. We made plans for me to pick him up in the morning, and I drove to Shelley's house for the night.

The following morning after stopping by to pick up Larry, I drove directly to my old doctor's office. When I'd called, the receptionist told me to stop by and she'd get me as soon as possible. Once inside the exam room, I told the Nurse Practitioner about the hysterectomy I had six weeks before Greg was diagnosed and how I wasn't able to get back in and see the doctor for my hot flashes and now I thought I had a UTI. I went on and told her about Greg dying and all about Sherry. I told her the whole story about Larry and how he was outside waiting for me and that we were on our way up to Orange County so he could meet Sherry. I alluded to the fact that I'd probably be having sex at some point in the future. She was kind and patient and very interested in my story. She didn't rush me. She reminded me of my sister, Cathy, the NP who I usually talked to about such things. She assured me that the urine test results were fine, but she wanted to examine me. She said that it was a good thing that I had come in because sex wasn't fun with an atrophied vagina. I was appalled to hear that I was atrophied; I had never heard of such a thing. She gave me a motherly smile, patted me on the shoulder and told me not to worry because the hormone patch and cream would work like a charm. She handed me some samples.

When I got back to the car, I told Larry what the nurse had said, then we had a good laugh over the fact that we both had learned something new about vaginas. I appreciated the comfort level I felt with Larry, being able to talk about such things without embarrassment.

Chris and the dogs met Larry and me at the front door. I rushed through the introductions because I couldn't wait to see Sherry. I was pleased to find her standing in the kitchen anxiously awaiting the big moment. She was feeling well, which was a relief to see after I had been gone for a day and a half. With all Larry's experience with oxygen tubes and cannulas, there wasn't a second of hesitation or intimidation on his part about giving her a hug.

Sherry looked me in the eye. "He's got your energy." She turned to Larry to explain. "As much as I loved my dad, his energy never matched my mom's. Well, at least, not until the end."

I stood there and gloated like a brand new mother; this was exactly what I wanted to see. The man I was falling in love with was experiencing Sherry's exacting honesty. I knew that, years down the road, Larry and I would relive this moment. Sherry wouldn't be a legend. This way there would be no misunderstanding. Thinking back now, it only makes sense why I had written what I did in my profile. I wanted him, whoever he was, to see for himself, to make his own decision about her.

For years, I had blamed my mother for forcing her opinions of my father on me, but now I realized that, with or without knowing it, my mother had actually been teaching me a valuable lesson. That's why I had never bought into anyone else's gossiping, complaining, bragging, or boasting about another person. I always wanted to make my own decisions about how I felt about someone. There are always two sides to every story, some weighing heavier with truth than the other, but nonetheless, those two sides always exist.

Numerous times Sherry and I had talked about how the ultimate test of Larry's character would be Olivia. Sherry's older dog, Rose, loved everyone, but Olivia was nervous and timid; she yapped even at people she knew, especially men. Within minutes, Olivia was sitting calmly in Larry's lap. Sherry and I smiled at each other. By that time, I didn't need anyone else's approval, but it was one more indication that all was well.

By late afternoon, Sherry finally grew tired after hours of visiting, eating, and flipping through her wedding album explaining to Larry who each family member was. Chris tucked her into her hospital bed. I marveled at what a huge success it had been, satisfied that we had seized the opportunity for Sherry and Larry to form their own opinions about each other.

I was elated by how well everything had gone, and anxious to move forward with the tentative plans that Larry and I had agreed on for that evening. Larry assured me that his family was on board with what was happening between us, but I wanted to see it for myself. We planned to meet his oldest daughter, Lisa, and her husband Cam, at a Chinese restaurant for an early dinner. I remembered how off kilter I felt after my mother died, and that had been over eighteen years ago. I couldn't imagine how Lisa must be feeling with all the hormonal changes of a three-month pregnancy and that it had only been four months since her mother had died.

Outside of the restaurant, the initial introductions went fine, but as soon as we were seated Lisa looked at me and said, "I'd like to know what your intentions are with my father."

I felt the blood rush to my face. I pulled my shoulders back. I thought about what Larry said to me the first time we met out in his driveway—he could spend the rest of his life with me. I blurted out with total confidence. "My intentions are to spend the rest of my life with him."

She put her hand up for a high-five. "Right on."

My shoulders relaxed. We all laughed. The ice had been broken and the rest of the evening my heart melted while Lisa talked about how much she loved and missed her mother, but how truly happy she was that her father and I had found each other.

During dinner, in the midst of talking about the work I had done for so long, Larry said, "I've never had a cavity." I was so impressed, and chuckled inside remembering how I had searched for any excuse—including "bad teeth"— not to send him my original communication.

After dinner Larry and I kissed and said our good-byes out in the parking lot. I went back home to Sherry's to be her "stay-at-home" mom, and he flew back to his vehicle in Texas.

It had only been three days since Larry had left, and I couldn't imagine my life without him. And in those same three days, I never imagined that Sherry could lose her breath so quickly. I thought I had prepared myself for everything, but I never expected that she would have to wear an oxygen mask. The mask, although child sized, covered most of her face. It made it difficult to understand what she was saying, so she would have to pull it down to her chin long enough to say what she wanted to say. On Saturday morning, Sherry seemed to be receiving and sending more text messages than usual. As soon as I was about to ask what was going on, she smiled and handed me her phone. It was Larry, sending her a text from his new phone. During the meeting, Larry had told Sherry all about what type he was going to get and she was so impressed by his technology knowledge.

Larry: *Hi Sherry, I hope you had a good night's sleep. Can you do me a favor? Give your mom a big hug & smile from me & let her know I love her. Thanks, Larry...PS. I love you, too.*

Sherry: *I will. Hope you have a great day. I will give her love from me from you. But I'm sure it won't be quite the same. Love, Sherry*

It was late Saturday night when I told Larry about Sherry's lack of oxygen and how she had just converted over to wearing the mask.

Before hanging up Larry said, "I have a question. What do you think about me coming straight home instead of driving up to Yellowstone?"

I hesitated. I knew what he was really saying—that the oxygen mask was a sign that the end might be near. I had the same dread myself. Something had shifted. "Oh, I don't know…." I sighed. My feelings were solid about Larry, but it was still complicated, because I still hadn't told anyone in Greg's family about him. Even in the best of circumstances, I knew it would be difficult, and these were not the best of circumstances. My love life wasn't just happening so soon after Greg's death; it was happening in a whirlwind while Sherry was dying. I couldn't imagine our standing around

Sherry's deathbed together—me and Larry, and Greg's parents.

"I don't want you to interrupt your trip for me," I said. I thought this would give me more time to figure it all out. Larry had told me from the beginning that he had planned on taking his mother to Yellowstone National Park before bringing her back home with him for a visit.

Larry said, "If I continue on my trip, I'd just be following the lines on the map that I drew two months ago...."

I cut him off. "But what about your mother's dream of seeing Old Faithful?"

"I've already talked to her; she's fine with my decision. She said that I should follow my heart. Yellowstone will always be there."

"I appreciate that, but I just don't know," I said.

"Think about it. I'll just need to know which direction to head by the time we get to New Mexico, and we'll be there tomorrow night. I'd really like to be there for you...to help in any way possible."

"I'll think about it, I promise."

I turned out the light. My mind drifted off to how comforting it would be to have Larry with me when Sherry slipped from this earth. When I had begged God to let Greg live longer, I had been completely focused on Greg's loving arms around me, and the solace of being loved even in the midst of death. But I didn't want to overreact. I mean, after all, Sherry was just wearing an oxygen mask. She was still fully functioning and alert. She could live another two weeks, or three, or a month. Then I thought about the promise I had made to Sherry just two years earlier, when we had first learned about her cancer: I would be there for her, doing anything she needed, until the very end. I had vowed, and the vow was anything *she* needed. This was Sherry's decision and had nothing to do with my wishes. I'd ask her in the morning so I could give Larry an answer. I had no idea what she would say. I drifted off to sleep and dreamt about Larry.

Chapter Fifteen

The Answer

THE FOLLOWING MORNING BEFORE my feet hit the floor, I set my intention of putting on a poker face. As much as I wanted to see Larry again, and as much as I wanted him there with me, I didn't want to influence Sherry's answer in any way. The last thing I wanted was for her to tell me yes because that's what she thought I wanted to hear. On the other hand, I prepared myself not to show any sign of disappointment if she said no. Besides, if she did say no, it wouldn't have been the end of the world. I knew that Larry's presence would be good for me, but it would just make things that much more complicated to have one more person in the mix.

When I came downstairs, I was relieved to see that Chris hadn't left for work yet. I could get both of their opinions and be done with it. So without any attachment to the outcome of their answer, I made my announcement. "Larry wants to come straight back home," I said.

Without a moment's hesitation, Sherry said, "Great." I looked at Chris, and he nodded in agreement with Sherry.

I was speechless. The last thing I expected was to have them both agree so quickly. I went to the kitchen and poured myself a cup of coffee.

Had they lost their minds? Obviously, they hadn't had a chance to give it any deep consideration. Didn't they know that if Larry were around that would mean that we'd have to introduce him to the hospice staff, or to anyone else who happened to be visiting Sherry? How could I possibly explain him?

I sighed watching the swirl of the coffee creamer float to the top. We'll see.

When I walked back to the family room, Sherry pulled the mask away from her face. "Mom, I think it would be good."

I glanced over at Chris hoping that he would save me by changing *his* mind, but he didn't.

Now that I knew how Sherry and Chris felt, I'd have to think about it some more on my own. What difference would it really make if Larry came back sooner? Sherry was dying. Nothing could make that okay. But was I just being selfish thinking of my own needs? Then I thought about what Larry had said on the phone last night—*He wanted to come back to help*.

There was one area where help was still needed. On different occasions, Sherry had told me how difficult it was going to be for Chris after she was gone. As much as Sherry had wanted me to move on with my life, she wanted Chris to do the same. But every time she mentioned it to him, he wouldn't hear anything of it. He'd scoff at her and say that he'd never, ever move on. This hung heavy on Sherry's heart. She told me that she feared for Chris's life. I'd been wondering if there was anything I could do to help Chris after she was gone, but when I asked Sherry, she said there wasn't, that the important thing was to take care of myself and that Chris would have to find his own way. She also told me to not feel hurt or to take it personally if Chris didn't call me after she was gone. I understood. Even though Chris and I had a good rapport, we really didn't have much in common, except for Sherry. But still, I was grateful to Chris that he had allowed me to live in his home and spend this time with Sherry. He was a good son-in-law, and a good husband to Sherry.

I thought about how comfortable and accepting Chris seemed to be about Larry, which had surprised me from the beginning. Even though Chris had been in our family for nine years, I saw him as shy and reserved. Knowing that men think and relate differently than women do, I thought if I couldn't help Chris directly, maybe Larry could. After all, Larry had recently lost his wife and Chris would soon enough be in the same situation. Their ages weren't that far off, since Chris was ten years older than Sherry and Larry was two and a half years younger than me. I thought that perhaps by seeing Larry's strength and courage to move on, Chris could see a ray of hope for his own future. More than ever, I was now able to see how life can and should go on.

It all made perfect sense to me, except for one thing. The thing I still couldn't shake. If Larry was around, how could I explain him to others? Would I introduce him as my new boyfriend? That sounded ridiculous to me. How could that have possibly happened so quickly? Besides this wasn't a time to talk about *me* and my love life. This was Sherry's time and no one else's.

For two and a half years, so many people—family, friends, and strangers—had been praying for Greg, for Sherry, for me, and our whole family. Prayer chains had been activated in churches that we had never attended. I wanted to share the good news with all those who had been praying, to tell them that their prayers had indeed brought one shining light into the darkness. But all of this would have to wait. First things first—I had to tell Greg's family.

Later that afternoon, I asked Sherry, again, about how and when to tell them. Her answer, as it had always been was,

"Wait. They're not ready yet."

"But when will they be ready?" I asked. I wanted to get it over with.

"Not yet." She coughed.

I wondered if Sherry was right. Larry and I had already talked about my in-laws because he had similar concerns about his.

A few hours later, Sue, the hospice nurse, came by. I told her my dilemma.

Sue looked at me and said, "Sherry should have anything she wants, be surrounded by those she wants, whatever it takes."

Then she turned to Sherry. "This is your final chance to ask for anything else you want."

Sherry and I looked at each other. We both knew what Sue meant; this was serious business and there was no time to waste. Sherry was quiet.

After Sue left, Sherry winked at me. "Have Larry come."

An hour later, when my mother-in-law called, I couldn't muster up the courage to talk to her right that minute, so I let it go to voicemail. I wanted to call her back to tell her that, at least in one area, things were better than they had been in a long time. But I told myself that the people who needed to know—specifically, my children and Larry's children—were all who mattered right now. I called my mother-in-law back and did my best to cheer her up without giving anything away. This was Sherry's time.

All evening, I kept thinking about how young I was feeling. The hot flashes that had plagued me had been drastically reduced—were almost gone—and I was feeling more centered and alive than I had been in a long time. I thought about what Sue had said about Sherry having her final chance to have things her way. I wondered what I'd do if it were my final chance, what it would feel like not to worry about what other people thought.

In bed that night, I read Sherry's words that I had placed next to Greg's urn.

It's Never—what if?
It's Always—thank God.
Moms are ordinary people
Doing extraordinary things

All of a sudden it dawned on me what she meant. It was time for me to quit worrying about all the "what ifs" in life. All I needed to do was accept what I had and thank God.

I settled into bed and called Larry. I had my answer for him—head straight home.

Larry was elated, and why not? All any of us want is to matter to the people we love, to be of service, to be asked to help. He would be back in less than twenty-four hours.

Before hanging up, I took a deep breath and asked for what I would ask for if I didn't care what anyone thought. "When you get back," I said, "I'd also like to go to a hotel."

I couldn't believe that I said it, but it was exactly the way I felt. I wanted to know what it would be like to lie next to him, to feel his body against mine all night long.

Larry said, "I'd love to, but are you sure? Do you understand the consequences?"

Of course, I knew what he was talking about. How would I feel if Sherry died while I was at a hotel with him? Would I be burdened with guilt the rest of my life? I knew this wasn't the time to bury my head in the sand; it was imperative that I had no regrets. I believed that I had already thought of every possible scenario and consequence, but I quickly agreed with Larry. I'd sleep on it. If I had missed something and had only said it because I was having a weak moment, certainly I'd come to my senses by morning.

Never in a million years did I think that eight hours later, I'd be confessing to Sherry that I wanted to go to a hotel with Larry. As close as I was to both of my daughters, I was still their mother, and we didn't talk about such intimate things.

Sherry's cheeks puffed up under the oxygen mask. Her eyes sparkled. "Are you gonna do it?"

I blushed. "Oh, I don't know, but it sure sounds nice. It doesn't mean...you know...that anything will happen. It would be nice."

Sherry pulled the mask down to her chin. "You should. It would be good for you. And you're free because it's Chris's days off."

Later that morning my mind was eased even more after Sherry handed me her phone to show me the text between her and Larry.

Sherry: *I'm happy to hear that you are coming home early. Now we will have more time to get to know each other better. Drive safe.*

Larry: *Thanks for saying that. I can't wait to see you.*

Against all odds, the man whom I had conjured out of the blue had not only formed a connection with me, but with my sweet Sherry, too. I felt overwhelmed with love for them both.

All day I thought about it. Sherry was right. It would be good for me to connect with Larry in this intimate way. In one of the earliest conversations, Larry and I talked about a book I had recently read called *The 5 Love Languages*. The book is about the five basic ways in which we relate to love, but it goes on to explain that everyone has a stronger preference toward one way: Words of Affirmation, Acts of Service, Physical Touch, Quality Time, or Gifts. Larry hadn't read the book, but he was curious enough that he stopped at a Books-A-Million store in Pensacola to buy it that same day. He read it over the next few nights. While he drove from New Orleans to Shreveport, we discussed the details of the book. Neither one of us were surprised that our main love language was physical touch and spending time together, because we had already talked about these things. We agreed that starting our relationship online was probably the best thing for us, as odd as that sounded. Since we're so physical, our emotions might have been clouded by touching. It was certainly different for both of us to start a relationship without touch. But now that we were sure, physical intimacy was the only natural progression.

So Tuesday morning, with all consequences considered, I made reservations at a nearby hotel for that night. I figured if Sherry took a turn for the worse, Larry and I could be back in minutes.

That evening, before Larry arrived to pick me up, one of the hospice counselors had come by for her periodic visit. Sherry was talking a mile a minute telling the counselor all about Larry and how I was going out to dinner with him.

I stood at the foot of Sherry's hospital bed and smiled.

The counselor's eyes darted back and forth between Sherry and me.

My shoulders tensed. I hoped and prayed that she didn't notice my overnight bag by the front door.

I knew exactly what she was thinking. How was it possible that things could have changed so quickly? Less than three weeks earlier, she knew me as a grieving widow, a mother whose sole purpose in life was to take care of her dying daughter. And now I was dressed up, ready to go out to dinner with some man I had met on a dating site.

This looked bad. I knew it.

But within seconds, things went from bad to worse when Sherry cheerfully told the counselor that I was going to spend the night with Larry.

In a heartbeat, I felt like a criminal. And without saying a single word the counselor folded her arms across her chest and became Judge Judy. I wanted to die.

I thought about explaining all the details of how and what happened and how I take things very seriously, but I could tell she wasn't in the mood to hear what I had to say—which made me want to tell her off. My heart pounded. My palms moistened. I wanted to tell her that just because she had her degree in counseling didn't mean that she knew it all. I wanted to tell her that if she knew anything about real love and the compassion that a mother feels for a daughter, she'd know that Sherry was all that mattered. I wanted to tell her to take her negative, judgmental, disapproving energy somewhere else because it was polluting my daughter's lungs.

But instead, I took a deep breath to calm myself down. I thought it would be easier to just call Larry and tell him not to come. Somehow I could explain to him that it was all just getting too complicated.

But as soon as I heard the doorbell ring, the tension in my body melted.

When Larry walked into the family room I totally relaxed. Seeing him again confirmed that I was doing exactly the right thing. It didn't matter what the counselor thought.

I was at peace. I introduced Larry to the counselor. I gave Sherry a hug and a kiss good-bye, and walked out of the room.

Larry and I had a nice dinner with wine. I told him how

relieved I was when he arrived at Sherry's door. He said he was relieved to see me. We talked about how I thought he could help Chris. He told me he would do everything in his power to help him. He pulled out his new iPhone and showed me the string of text messages with Sherry a few days earlier.

Larry: Hi Sherry I hope you're having a great day. It was so nice meeting you on Wednesday. Thanks for having me in your lovely home. You and Chris are a great couple! I can't wait to see you when I return.

Sherry: Thanks. It was nice to meet you too. It's nice to have a new texting phone right? Now we need Mom to get one. Text me anytime. Have a great day. Love, Sherry

Larry: I'll show her mine when I get back, I'm sure she will love it

Sherry: Show her what when you get back? Love, Sherry

Larry: My new phone

Sherry: Oh I was wondering. :) Love, Sherry

Larry: I'm trying to be/act appropriate. :) Love, Larry

Sherry: Glad one of us is mature.

Larry: So you are the one out of the three of us. Neither your Mom nor I have been acting very mature lately.

Sherry: That's ok. You're having fun and you both deserve it.

Larry: Thanks, you are as sweet as your Mom.

Sherry: I try. Love, Sherry

I laughed until I cried. I thought—that little stinker!

Larry and I held hands across the table. When we looked up, the restaurant was empty.

Once inside the hotel room, it was beautiful and honest, but as sure as we were about each other, it suddenly felt very strange to be with someone different. We slowly felt our way. We laughed. We cried. We talked. We longed for familiarity. We explored some more. We lay, belly to back, and then turned back to belly. It was surreal.

Several hours later, I went to the bathroom. I screamed.

Larry bolted out of bed and knocked on the door. "Are you okay in there?"

I sighed as loud as I could. "Yeah…you didn't put the toilet seat down." In twenty-five years I never had to check it; Greg had always put it down.

When I came out, Larry looked dismayed. He said, "You know…these are the shitty times. It's gonna get better."

I smiled; I knew exactly what he meant. If given the

choice, we would've kept life the way it had been, and, really, that would have been awesome, because there's nothing better than history, than familiarity, than knowing the toilet seat will be down. But one guarantee in life is that change will happen, whether we want it to or not.

Early the following morning, I woke up with exactly what I wanted—Larry's body curled around mine. I felt more connected and grounded; I was satisfied that I had taken the next step toward creating my new life. I lay there daydreaming about how much fun it would be to have Larry's daughters meet Sherry and Charlotte. I thought back to the summer when Greg and I dated and how much fun it was to take all four kids to the beach, the Padres games, and Balboa Park. Of course, I understood that it would be different. We would all have to meet at Sherry's and hang around her hospital bed. But it could still be lots of fun to see how our daughters interacted with each other. After meeting Lisa, I was confident that Charlotte and Sherry would love her and besides, four young women can always find something to talk about.

Larry stroked my arm. "You know, Gina will be coming out in two weeks. Wouldn't it be cool if we could get all of our girls in the same room? Maybe we could have a pizza party."

I couldn't believe that we were having such similar thoughts. I kissed him. I jumped out of bed. I could hardly wait to get back to Sherry's and apologize for all the times I thought how silly and childish she was for believing in Prince Charming. I couldn't wait to see what she thought about having a pizza party.

Chapter Sixteen

The Gift of Acceptance

LATER THAT MORNING, AFTER Larry and I arrived back at Sherry's, I was thankful to see that she was full of energy and more talkative than usual. She agreed that the pizza party sounded like a great idea. Then she showed me her calendar. It was lined up for days; everyone wanted to see her. She had her dear high school friend, Julie, coming in from out of state to stay for a few days. It was so sweet, but I also hoped the visitors wouldn't wear Sherry out. I wanted her for myself.

But then reminded myself that this was Sherry's time to have whatever she wanted, to see whomever she wanted.

I had to let go.

On Friday morning, Sherry collapsed in the hallway while coming out of the bathroom. She struggled to get her breath and was unable to get herself up off the floor. Fortunately, her friend Julie was there, and between the two of us we were able to get her back into bed. I thought it was the end, but she rallied, although not completely. Later that afternoon, after Julie left, Sherry slept for several hours, which was unusual for her during the day.

Charlotte and Stuart arrived the next morning. If I were to get at least part of my wish of getting our families together, I'd better speak up. We couldn't wait two more weeks for Gina to arrive. Later that afternoon, I brought the subject up with Charlotte to see how she felt about meeting Larry and his family.

"Of course," she smiled. "Let's set it up for tomorrow morning."

I hugged and held onto her tighter and longer than usual. I knew what a difficult time it was for her. I was so grateful and, again, amazed how open, loving, and selfless she was to allow me to have such a gift.

On Sunday morning, when Larry, Lisa, Cam, and Larry's mother, Bobbie, arrived, we didn't serve pizza, but it felt like a party anyway. There were individual conversations going on like they do at a cocktail party. I wanted to listen in on everyone's story, but it was impossible. So most of the time I sat back and took in the scene that I knew would never happen again. For a while Lisa, Charlotte, and Bobbie were gathered around Sherry's hospital bed chattering and laughing while Chris, Larry, Cam, and Stuart were talking. Then Larry joined in a conversation with Charlotte and Sherry, while Lisa showed me some of her wedding photos. But there was one moment when everyone got drawn in together.

Sherry pulled her mask down and said, "I'm so glad that our parents have found each other."

"Me, too," Lisa said. Then she laughed. "But my dad broke his family rule. He never allowed my sister or me to communicate with anyone online. But I did anyway, and that's how I met Cam."

Larry chimed in, "Yea, after Lisa met such a great guy, how could I be against dating sites?"

"Well at least not against eHarmony," Charlotte said.

Everyone laughed.

The following day, Larry and I had some much needed alone time with Sherry to broach the subject that we needed to talk to her about.

Larry pulled a chair up closer to Sherry's bedside. "I wanted to talk to you about your funeral and whether or not I should go. Your mother and I have talked about what we felt was appropriate, but I wanted to get your take on it."

Sherry reached out for Larry's hand.

Sherry listened intently as Larry and I took turns running

through the different options that we had previously discussed. If Larry sat next to me in the front pew everyone would be wondering who in the heck this man was with his arm around me as I was sobbing on his shoulder. We all quickly agreed that having him sit next to me would just be too awkward. We thought another option would be to have Larry sit in the back of the church and pretend that he didn't know me. Of course, the three of us quickly agreed that would be creepy. Another option would be to introduce him as a family friend. No, that wouldn't work; there was too much chemistry. Anyone who was in the same room could spot it a mile away. It left us with no good options. A funeral just wasn't the time or place to introduce Larry.

Sherry pulled down her oxygen mask. "I agree. It's not gonna work, but believe me I know how much you care." She brought the mask back up, took in a few breaths, pulled it down to her chin again. "I'm just so happy you're here for my mom. Thank you."

Larry leaned in and gave Sherry a hug. "I've heard what your dad's instructions were. I promise you that I will always comfort your mother and make sure that she has fun."

I was amazed and deeply touched that Larry had remembered the specific details of Greg's wishes. I had mentioned it during one of our conversations. Sherry knew exactly what Larry was talking about because she and I had many conversations about how sweet it was that Greg had written out these specifics in one of his journals soon after he was diagnosed.

Sherry wiped away her tear. "Thank you, Larry."

Larry said, "I love your mother. Thank you for everything you've done in getting us together. You truly are an angel."

I took in a deep breath. I thought about the similarities of what Greg and Sherry wanted towards the end. They both wanted some kind of reassurance that I was going to be okay. Another thing that struck me as odd was how they had both told me, on two separate occasions, that the hardest part of dying was that they were going to miss me so much. I thought about how far I had come and how much they had both taught me. Their ability to be so open and honest with me gave me the ability to listen and accept.

I was at complete peace with all that we discussed. I could think of only one thing that we had missed.

When should I tell Greg's family about Larry?

I had already asked Sherry so many times. I wasn't going to bother her with it again. I would figure it out on my own.

By the following night, two weeks after I had first met Larry in person, it was clear Sherry was getting closer to the end. Significantly weaker, she could no longer make it to the restroom. We had a portable potty next to her bed. She wasn't engaging in conversations, just a few words here and there. It was mainly the squeezing of hands and fluttering of her eyes. Chris and I agreed we should start holding 24-hour vigilance over her. With the help of hospice, we had a full team: Larry, Chris's sister, Stacey, Charlotte, and Stuart. Sherry rested peacefully while we stayed by her side and administered medication to keep her comfortable. On the third night, I slept on the couch closest to Sherry's hospital bed and Chris sat by all night. As strange as it seems, before I went to sleep I prayed for the end to come. I wished her the ultimate peace.

In the wee hours the next morning, I could hear Sherry struggling to pull the mask away from her face. She said, "I don't want you to commit suicide...on me."

I shot up. My eyes met Chris's. *What did she mean?*

Chris asked, "What are you talking about?"

Sherry became agitated. "I don't want you to commit suicide," she said firmly.

I finally understood. Sherry was still hanging on because she wanted to be positive that Chris was going to be okay. If it's humanly possible to feel someone else's "*aha*" moment, I experienced Chris's. He understood and promised Sherry that he wouldn't commit suicide, and he meant it.

All three of us relaxed. I thought for sure that Sherry's time to die would be very soon. She was ready, and so were Chris and I. But it didn't happen. Later that afternoon, it became clear that she had the same thought. Charlotte, Stuart, Chris, and I were hovering around her bed when Sherry woke up frustrated and said, "Why can't I just die?"

By Sunday night, everyone was exhausted. Larry and I had the most energy, because that's what happens when you're falling in love. Everyone else went upstairs to sleep while Larry and I held our first vigil together. We settled in the two Queen Anne chairs next to her bedside. I held Sherry's hand and Larry was down by her feet. At first, I wondered if Larry and I would sit there in silence while we watched over her, but before long we began talking about our future plans, normal everyday stuff. I never thought I would be so relaxed to talk about such seemingly insignificant things while Sherry was in her final stages of dying. But she was so peaceful. She didn't have the death rattle that Greg had in his last hours, which made me think how I'd heard that a dying person can hear and feel the energy of those around them, even though they can't respond.

It was close to midnight when Larry asked me how I liked to decorate my house. Since my house was rented out at the moment, Larry had no idea what my house looked like. I was delighted that he cared. It was easy to explain what I liked because Sherry and I had similar taste. I pointed around the room at all the things Sherry had picked out for her house—the different shades of green in the floral valances that she had sewn, the cream colored leather couches and the chairs that we were sitting on. I pointed to a few things I didn't like so much—the floral urn that she had bought online for Chris to keep her ashes in and the fake bird she had perched in the silk ficus tree. I was getting wrapped up into all the details of the new home I would soon be making.

About forty-five minutes into our conversation, Larry said, "Her breathing has changed."

I leaned in closer to watch her chest rise and fall. *How could I not have noticed?* I was so grateful that Larry had pointed it out. The change was slight.

Larry touched my shoulder. "I think you should go wake

everyone up," he said.

My heart pounded. I raced up the stairs and woke up Chris, Charlotte, and Stuart. We came down quickly, stood around Sherry, holding our breath as she took in several more of her own.

And then she stopped.

We all looked at each other, stunned and amazed by her timing. I know I should have been feeling utterly devastated in that moment, but for some unknown reason, I didn't. I felt relieved that if God had to take her, at least he allowed her to die a "good death" surrounded by her family.

Chris removed her mask. Larry turned off the oxygen concentrators.

It was so good to see Sherry's whole face again—so young and serene.

I said my good-bye and stayed close by to comfort Charlotte while she said hers. It broke my heart that she had lost her little sister. Charlotte and I embraced each other like we had never done before. We were there for each other. Then she took a seat next to Stuart on one couch, and I sat beside Larry on the other one. Chris stayed by Sherry. When I felt Larry's arm slip around me, it brought me great solace. I thought about how happy Sherry must have been to hear Larry and I talking about how we would decorate our house someday, something she and I would have talked about for hours. The reality of never being able to have such a conversation with her again hadn't hit me yet.

After everyone had said their personal good-byes, I hadn't

planned on it, but I instinctively took the lead. A formal prayer didn't feel right. Sobbing and wailing over her body was out of the question because that would not have made her happy. But I thought how she would love it if I read what she had written. It had brought her such great comfort—Sherry's Gift of Acceptance. I knew exactly where it was on her hospital tray table. I picked it up, settled back on the couch next to Larry and read it aloud. I didn't cry or stumble. It was my honor.

Sherry's Gift of Acceptance

I have the gift to accept the things that cannot be changed. Having this gift allowed me to reconnect with old friends, and meet new friends as well. This gift gave me the ultimate blessings of being able to be with Chloe [her dog that died one and a half years earlier] when she needed me, and Mom and Dad when they needed me. This gift also allowed me to inspire people.

Along with acceptance comes freedom. Freedom to see the true blessings in our lives. Freedom to see the bigger picture (which is the ability to see the blessings). For one door doesn't close without another one opening. The biggest blessing acceptance brings is peace.

This applies to every aspect in our lives.

Acceptance is forgiveness.

Acceptance is positive energy.

Acceptance is love of yourself and everyone else, too.

Do not judge. Change what needs to be changed.

Keep company with those who lift your spirit, who bless your life and who you can help in some way. Do not change them, for they are on their journey of acceptance. But be an example of acceptance and show them the blessings it has brought you, and the peace it continues to bring.

Accept people for who they are.

I have always believed in having a purpose for being on this earth. I call it our divine life purpose. I believe that when we figure out what that is and we do this, we are happier, more peaceful and closer to God. I believe that my life purpose is having the ability to accept the things I cannot change. My journey with cancer has brought this to my attention even stronger, even though I can think of hundreds of examples of this throughout my life. I have also always believed in "a bigger picture," meaning that everything happens for a reason, and that when we die we will know what that is. People have asked me many times why I have been so "OK" with all of this and my answer is because I know that this is part of a bigger plan. But now I think I know what the bigger picture is, at least for me. My acceptance of this disease has brought forth so many blessings in my life and the GIFT from God that I get is to know them now, cherish them and share them with others while I am still alive.

Knowing that I have a divine purpose has given me great comfort, peace and joy.

Thank you, Mom. And thank you, God, who gave her the inspiration to explain what my purpose was. This has been the greatest gift anyone could have ever given me.

After I read it, I thought we needed a little humor, so I asked Chris to read Sherry's final list. I had already seen it and had chuckled inside, just like I did when she was a young girl when her list would say: Wake up. Go to the bathroom. Get dressed.

Chris loved lists as much as Sherry. In a clear, loud voice he read:

1) Call Hospice.
2) Tell them I died.

We laughed. And then we cried.

Although I was already missing her, part of me felt like a feather floating in the breeze. I would be okay, because feathers fall lightly. The floating feeling was also Sherry's soul ascending into the heavens. The biggest part of me felt solid, stronger, and for that I was grateful. God had orchestrated everything in his perfect plan.

My sweet Sherry had lived and died perfectly.

Chapter Seventeen

Good-Bye

THE DAY BEFORE SHERRY'S funeral, I kissed Larry good-bye and drove up to Orange County to meet all the out-of-town family and friends who would be staying at the same hotel. While I sat in the traffic on I-5, I thought back to the argument that Sherry and Chris had over what kind of service she should have and how much anger I felt that night. Now, it eased my mind that no more precious time had been wasted arguing about the details of her funeral. And since

Chris had it his way, he and his family took full responsibility for making all of the arrangements, and I didn't have to worry about a thing.

When I arrived in the hotel lobby, Sherry's grandmother Betty was waiting there for me. She had always felt like a mother to me. When she had come out from Arizona several months earlier to visit Sherry, I felt a different kind of connection to her. Betty had been widowed for several years and her son, my ex-husband Bob, had recently passed away. His hard life of drinking and drugs had finally caught up with him. We reminisced about Sherry, but it was impossible for me to talk about Sherry without bringing up Larry. I bubbled over with excitement and told Betty all the details about how I came to meet him—how instrumental Sherry had been in making it happen. Betty was a salt-of-the-earth kind of woman who always spoke her mind. Her eyes sparkled and she laughed. "Hey, I have no interest in finding another man, but for you…why not. Life's short."

The following morning when I arrived at the church, I sat in the front pew where I had sat nine years earlier when Sherry and Chris were married. Waves of emotion came over me. My heart was being ripped out of my chest. I refused to let her go. In the next breath, an eeriness crept in. *Was this really me sitting at my sweet Sherry's funeral?* No, it couldn't be. Then, for what seemed like an eternity, I sat there in a fog, staring at the large framed photo of Sherry at the altar. It was all a blur—the flowers, the people, the prayers, the music, the emptiness in the church without her, and without Larry. To save myself from drowning, I had to bring her back. So I let my mind drift back to her wedding day—that wonderful day when I watched Greg walk her down that same aisle. She was the most beautiful bride I had ever seen. Then I thought about how Greg and Sherry wanted me to move on with my life, and so did I. I made up my mind then, that in order to completely move on, I had to tell Greg's parents about Larry. An excitement rose inside me. I was finally free to share my good news with the world.

Following the formal church service, Chris's parents opened their lovely home for a celebration of Sherry. There was a beautiful spread of food and floral arrangements. Everyone gathered around the big screen to watch the DVD of photos and music that Charlotte and her friend Daphne had put together of Sherry's life from the beginning to the end. When the video ended, I pulled Greg's father to the side to ask him if he would gather some of the family together to meet me at the hotel—I had some good news to share. I was always more of a one-on-one person, but my father-in-law liked big family announcements, so he quickly agreed. I thought, Why not share the good news with the whole family? Didn't falling in love warrant such attention?

After returning back to the hotel, Charlotte, Stuart, and nine of Greg's family members gathered in the conference room. I took a deep breath and told them the whole story. They surrounded me with warm congratulations. Now I was really free to move on.

My sister Diana had decided not to come out for Sherry's funeral. Instead, she came the following week to stay with Larry and me for five days. Growing up, Diana had always protected me, but now she was like a mother bear on steroids. Even though she had been married for decades, she was a fiercely independent woman who had very little tolerance for women who were dependent on any man. She was bound and determined to come up with a reason to dislike Larry and give me her opinion. The third night, after we got into bed, Larry whispered, "She's relentless—a drill sergeant." Evidently, each morning while I was still sleeping, Diana and Larry, being early risers, would drink coffee for several hours while she grilled him.

The next afternoon, Diana and I were out lounging in the pool. She looked at me and said, "Well, all I can say is—you won the Lottery."

I smiled.

After Diana left, I began to write. When I wrote, I cried, but I couldn't stop writing about Greg and Sherry.

Chapter Eighteen

Building Trust

LARRY AND I DISCUSSED our feelings and beliefs about cremation. What would eventually happen to the ashes? When the keepers passed on, would the ashes be thrown out by someone who didn't care or know what they were? When Sherry shopped on Amazon to order a large floral urn for Chris and asked me to pick out two smaller ones, one for me and one for Charlotte, I didn't have the heart to tell her that I didn't want her ashes. I wanted her. So I picked out two of the smallest urns I could find to respect her wishes.

Larry told me how Rosemary and he had agreed that their ashes would be scattered at the same location at sea. I liked that idea. I wished Greg and I had thought of something like that. I remembered how overwhelmed I felt when the funeral attendant said I needed to pick out an urn for Greg's. That day Sherry waited while I looked over all the different types—none of them moved me. I picked one that looked like a small flying saucer.

Larry stroked my arm and said, "You know it's realistic to think that we could be together longer than I was with Rosemary and you were with Greg. What do you think about scattering Greg's ashes where Rosemary's are? Then I would fulfill my promise to her and then someday, we would all be together in the same place."

I glanced over at Greg's urn sitting on top of Rosemary's dresser: it looked so out of place. I had done everything that he had requested, scattered some on the golf course, and wore some in a locket close to my heart. I thought about how much he loved the ocean. Larry's suggestion sounded like the perfect solution. So we made all the arrangements to do it on the first anniversary of Greg's death.

The afternoon we arrived at the boat dock, Greg's ashes were in a basket covered with rose petals. The captain of the boat took Larry and me out to the same location off Pacific Beach where he had released Rosemary's ashes five months earlier. We both smiled when we saw one lone duck watching as the boat idled.

I knelt by the side of the boat next to the basket of Greg's ashes and paused. I listened carefully while Larry read the words he had written for Rosemary and Greg. I was impressed by not only his strength, but the amount of respect that he showed equally to Rosemary and Greg.

He read:

Rosemary,

You were my wife, lover, confidant, and best friend for 32 years. You brought me untold happiness and joy. Now you are with our maker, I'll join you in the future. As you know, in the mean time I've found a new earthly mate. I know you approve of her as I've already seen the signs you've sent me. Thanks for all you did for me. I love you.

Greg,

We never had the opportunity to meet, but I feel as if I know you because I can see the influence you had on Rhonda. You were always focused and driven and you instilled that in her. I've read your notes on what you want for Rhonda and I'm ready to take on that mission. I promise I'll follow your wishes and take care of her for the rest of my life. Peace be with you, my friend. I'll see you later.

I bravely released Greg's ashes along with the rose petals into the deep blue Pacific. I told him how much I loved him and that I'd join him someday.

On the way back to the boat dock, the sun had dipped a little lower in the sky and the air had cooled. Larry pulled his iPhone out and wrapped his other arm around my shoulder. I was surprised to hear, "You Are," Greg's and my song. Then he played "Babe," Rosemary's and his favorite song. We kissed as the boat docked. All four of us became connected as one.

One day in early September, Larry suggested that we drive to Texas, pick up his mother and take her to Yellowstone. I wondered if he had remembered reading Sherry's note that she had sent with me the first time I met him in person: *Bring up the issue that you're a* _nervous_ *passenger* _in the car!_ I never understood where my deep-seated fear of being a passenger in a vehicle came from, but it was something that had caused me a lot of grief since I was a child. One would have thought that I had been in a head-on collision and barely survived, but I had only been in a few fender benders. Sherry and I had many conversations trying to figure out where my unfounded fears had come from. Unable to reach any reasonable conclusions, we settled on the idea that maybe I had died in a car crash in a previous life.

Bob and Greg had complained about me asking them to be careful or slow down, which eventually turned into me keeping my mouth shut and holding on for dear life. But I wanted to be with Larry, so I agreed to go on the trip. Everything was fine until we were winding our way up on the road that led to Yellowstone. It was early October. The first snow had just begun to fall. I gripped the seat as the yellow line disappeared, feeling the avalanche of my road fears building up inside of me.

Larry said, "Are you okay?"

I couldn't believe that he cared—that he noticed. Yet a familiar guilt tugged at me. I was certain to be reprimanded for my fear. I said, "Oh, it's just me."

But Larry persisted, and I was so relieved. "I'd really like to help. Do you want me to go slower?"

I felt a sudden lightness. "Yes." That's what I had always wanted, but Greg and Bob never listened.

Larry immediately slowed down, and I exhaled through my parted lips.

Standing at the lookout, the snowcapped Tetons were breathtaking. Bobbie and I hugged when Old Faithful spewed its steam high into the crisp air. Larry took tons of photos. The three of us got along famously. Everything was beautiful, but nothing was more magnificent than being heard and feeling safe.

I was almost sad when the trip was over, but we needed to get home to host a baby shower for Lisa.

Chapter Nineteen

Sherry's Sign

I SUPPOSE IT'S COMMON for most of us to look for some kind of sign—anything to assure us that our loved one hasn't completely abandoned us—that they're ok. For some, it's a feather floating out of nowhere, or a bluebird perched in a tree. For others, it may be a dream or a strong feeling that comes on suddenly. I'm sure there are as many different signs as there are people.

From the beginning, Lisa and Larry had both talked about how excited they were that her due date was on Larry's birthday—the 21st. Lisa's unexpected pregnancy so soon after her mother's passing was a sign, they thought. And whenever we heard the Eagles' song "Hotel California," her favorite, we thought of her. Rosemary had bonded with two mallard ducks that came up from the lake and hung out by their back door. She'd fed them for months and named them Harold and Maude. Now whenever we came across a pair of ducks, Lisa would raise her eyebrows and laugh and say, "There's Harold and Maude again."

Before Sherry died, I asked her if she would send me signs.

She smirked through her oxygen mask and rolled her eyes. "Look for a yellow balloon," she said. A yellow balloon? I was disappointed that she didn't take me more seriously. I wanted something profound that equaled her.

The day after her funeral, Larry and I were driving south on I-5. We saw a solid yellow hot air balloon off to the left not too far away. I was ecstatic.

I quietly held on to the idea that Rose would not be born on Larry's birthday, but on Sherry's, the 23rd. I didn't necessarily think that it would be a sign, but I saw it as a way of bringing back a part of Sherry.

When Larry answered the phone in the wee hours of the morning of the 21st, I thought for certain Rose had arrived.

Larry was bouncing off the wall with excitement. I was happy and excited for him and for Lisa. But I also had a sense of disappointment and guilt. How could I be so concerned over this? Why was this so important to me? I shook off my emotions, and got ready to head to the hospital.

Then, before Larry and I could even get out the door, the phone rang again. I saw the letdown on his face. "Don't bother coming," Lisa told him. "They're sending me home. They'll induce tomorrow morning at 8."

My spirits lifted. "Since we're up, why don't we go out to breakfast?" I asked Larry. Going out to breakfast wasn't my favorite thing to do, but it brought back the smile to Larry's face. We drove to the IHOP around the corner and held hands across the table. Every time the waitress would come around to refill our coffee, we'd tell her bits and pieces about our story. With each new thing she learned, she lingered longer and smiled wider. It was exactly what I wanted to see, not only for us, but for her as well.

Before long our waitress had planted herself at our table. She wanted to know all the details, just like Sherry's dental hygiene classmates. So I started from the beginning, telling her about Sherry wanting me to "get a life." It was so much fun to share the good news that I did get a life. And how blessed we were that another new life was on her way!

The following morning, the 22nd, when Larry and I arrived at the hospital, they'd started Lisa's IV drip. Lisa smiled and said, "I'm so ready to hold Rose in my arms." Cam was video-taping and narrating everything that was happening: "Rose, this is your Mommy while she's in labor with you." Then he pointed the camera at me. "And this is your Grandma, Rhonda." My heart melted. It no longer mattered what day Rose was born on. This would be the perfect day.

I thought about when I held Charlotte and Sherry for the first time. I was the one who reassured and comforted them. And before I knew it they were young girls, and then grown women, who reassured and comforted me. I couldn't wait to cradle Rose in my arms, to hold her little hand, and sing Braham's "Lullaby" in her ear.

By mid-afternoon, things still weren't moving along with Lisa's labor. The on-call doctor looked at Larry and me and said, "You might as well go home. It's gonna be closer to midnight."

Midnight? Maybe this would be a sign from Sherry! Something profound.

So Larry and I drove back home to wait for another call. On the way, I thought about similarities between birth and death. No matter how smart we think we are, only God knows when life will begin and end. We cry when our loved ones leave this world, but they smile because they're going to the other side. A baby cries when she enters this world, and we smile because the little one is here. I remembered Sherry's face when I asked her if she'd send me a sign. Was she mocking me because I had so little faith? I thought about the phrase "Let go. Let God," realizing that it's all about love and trust, how much more I needed to learn.

We got the final call at 9:30 AM on Sherry's birthday. "She's starting to push," Cam said. "They'll do a C-section if the baby's not here by noon."

"We're on our way," Larry and I said in unison.

When we arrived, Lisa looked tired but still strong.

"Lisa really wanted you to be here," the doctor said, and smiled at me. "She's just told me the whole amazing story and that today's Sherry's birthday."

I was deeply touched by the acceptance and love I felt from Lisa and the fact that she'd shared our story with her doctor.

A C-section was decided on. Cam, Larry, and I followed the gurney as the doctor wheeled Lisa through the operating room doors. Larry and I glanced at each other with wide eyes. Doctors don't wheel gurneys. It felt like the red carpet was being laid out for us all. The doctor nodded to Larry and me and said, "Don't go to the waiting room, wait here. This is where the nurse will be bringing the baby out right after she's born."

Twenty minutes later, the nurse wheeled Rose out in a bassinet and paused. "Meet your beautiful granddaughter before she gets weighed and bathed." I leaned into Larry, unable to take my eyes off Rose's tiny nose and sweet little lips. I let out a sigh, unable to hold my tears back any longer. Larry and I followed alongside the bassinet as the nurse rolled the baby down the hallway into the nursery. We held onto each other as we peered through the window watching Rose. Another angel had just been born.

After Lisa was transferred into a private room, Larry and I went down to the cafeteria to grab some lunch. We both felt like we were floating. How was it possible to be this happy, especially in a hospital cafeteria? Between us we'd eaten in so many, for so many years. It was like the night that Sherry and I watched Cinderella's Castle light up at Disney World. "Silent Night, Holy Night" filled the room, poinsettia centerpieces on each table.

Like Sherry, my angel, said after I read her the words I tacked onto my dating profile, "Perfect, Mom, perfect."

Sherry, born 12:53 PM, December 23, 1973
Rose, born 12:35 PM, December 23, 2009

Sherry's
Good-Bye Letter

My Dearest Mom,

This is the most difficult letter that I have ever written. My love for you is immeasurable, selfless, and unconditional. I know your love for me is the same. I am blessed to have a mom who fulfills all of my needs. There has never been a time in my life when I have questioned your love for me, or the sacrifices you made for me. It is through you that I have grown into the person that I am today. It was through watching you change and grow that enabled me to grow and to learn how to become a better person. When you changed, I changed.

You have been so selfless to me since the day I was born. You have given up so much for me throughout my life, and I want to say Thank you for being so unconditionally loving to me. I only hope that you know how grateful I am for all you have done for me. All your selflessness did not go unnoticed. I know how hard it was for you to have to raise two young girls, work and try to be the best mother around. Even though I didn't get to physically see you very much then, I always knew and felt your love.

When I was little and we lived in Arizona, I remember being outside all the time. I was climbing trees, riding my bike, playing tetherball, catching bugs and playing with my cats and dogs. I missed you a lot. You were at work so many hours but I would be so happy when you got home. I remember watching you sit in the bathroom sink to put your makeup on. You would stand on one leg when you cooked. You would make us interesting things to eat like spaghetti squash. Nobody made mac-n-cheese like you did. You tried to perm my hair once, and you were always curling it for me because I was obsessed with having it curly. You would put pink curlers in it before bedtime. I never remember you being upset with me. When I was a teenager you gave me a Sucrets box and said, "Don't tell Charlotte."

When we moved to California I was happy because I was able to spend a lot more time with you. Unfortunately, you were usually a lot more stressed and busy in other ways. I was really proud of you getting your AA degree. You always said that education was something nobody could take away from you. You encouraged me to go to college and make something of myself. The day I graduated from Hygiene School, I don't know who was more proud, you or me. I was excited to work with you at the office. Lunch time was great because we could catch up on what was going on in our lives. But, after the commute got to me, I started working for Chris. This wasn't good because I was unhappy and so were you because we missed each other. So we made dates to see each other more. Then you moved to Arizona. I was so mad at Dad for taking you there that I felt like I didn't ever want to talk to him again. So I stopped calling, but all that did was punish you and me.

When Dad got diagnosed with the cancer that had gone to his brain, I was happy you would be moving back to California. Also, Dad had changed his ways, and he had become the new wonderful, sweet, loving Dad. I had the best of both worlds. The perfect mother and a great dad, who after all these years was treating her like she deserved. Please honor me by moving on and having a wonderfully happy life. Write your book and work on your business if that makes you happy.

I am looking forward to the day when I will see you again in Heaven. I will be waiting with open arms.

I Will Always Love You,
Sherry, July, 2009

Epilogue

THE FOLLOWING MAY, LARRY and I were married on a ship, with family and close friends joining us for a three-day cruise to Mexico. Charlotte walked me down the aisle. I was never so happy, not only for myself, but for her, because she had also gained a new family. Larry's daughters, Lisa and Gina, met us at the end of the aisle and together all three of our daughters gave us their blessings.

For the first several years, it was awkward when someone who didn't know me would ask me if I had children, because

I feared their next question. Where do they live? But after Charlotte and Stuart moved to Hawaii I decided to come right out and say it. "I have two daughters. One lives in Paradise, the other one lives in Heaven."

Almost three years after Sherry died, all of a sudden I felt like I hit a brick wall. I grieved more than usual for Sherry and for Greg. I regretted that I had told his family about Larry so soon after Sherry's funeral, because in the end there were some hurt feelings over the timing of my announcement. *Was it really an appropriate time? Or was it grief?* Confused, I cried all day. I couldn't write. The last thing anyone needed was more pain and grief. I wondered if this is what the hospice counselor meant when she said grief can strike at any time, even years later.

I called hospice and met with a wonderful counselor, Gail. She asked if I wanted to explore something she called Sandplay Therapy. There's no right or wrong way, she assured me. Just use the figurines and sand to create anything that comes to you. I looked over at the bookcases filled with hundreds of miniature figurines. It reminded me of the hobbyist collections you would see at a County Fair.

Thinking about Sherry, I gathered all the Disney characters and placed them in the sandbox. She would have loved it. For Greg, I loaded my arms with the sports figurines. I gathered all the dogs, for me and Sherry. I spotted an owl on the shelf and thought about Rosemary, who loved owls. My mother came to mind when I saw the little Christmas Village house at the back of the shelf. Gail watched me and took notes; I imagined she was pleased with my box. I grabbed about twenty more items and placed them into the sand. The box was so full. I had stuffed animals hanging over the edges. I had only shed a few tears.

But when I went home and Googled "Sandplay Therapy," I saw very simple boxes, with only a few items. I felt embarrassed.

Two weeks later, in her office, I asked Gail why my sandbox tray was filled with so much stuff when the ones I had seen online were so simple. She explained that perhaps it was the enormity of my experiences and feelings that had come "flooding" into the box. I sat there for a moment and acknowledged all that I had lost. That made sense.

Several days later, I noticed what felt like a life raft under me. I was no longer sinking, but instead I was rising up to meet my divine purpose. I came to realize more of what Sherry meant by saying that she wanted me to "get a life." It was not simply about wanting me to find a man to love. That was the easy part. I already knew how to love a man.

What she wanted, for me, was to seek and find and trust myself, and to let go of worrying about what people might think. I had to tell my whole story, my way, to inspire others never to give up hope of finding love and peace themselves, no matter what adversities they might face. It doesn't matter what kind of love we find, as long as it's DEEP and WIDE and REAL. For some, it may be a new romantic love; for others, it might be a renewal of love in their marriage. Perhaps it could be a strengthening of love between a parent and child, or simply learning how to love oneself. I did all of the above. At the end of the day, all we really need is LOVE.

If I were to make a sandbox today, I would be quiet, still. I would go deep inside and place two, maybe three items in the box. One would represent whatever I needed to work on at that time, whatever felt out of balance. The other item would be a heart of some kind. It would represent the love and hope that always existed in my life. There's no doubt that Sherry, Greg, and Rosemary are all smiling down from heaven on our new family.

Today, Larry and I have our fifth grandchild—five in five years—Lisa has three girls and Gina has two boys. We see and play with them frequently, we travel, and we're creating our own history as we develop new friendships along the way. A few months after Sherry died, Larry sold his half of his remodeling business to his partner. He took a year off. Now he's living his dream of buying and rehabbing houses. It's a joy to help him with design, paint colors, and granite choices.

My writing has helped me to grieve—to let go—and at the same time to hold Greg and Sherry near. God has blessed me with the strength and courage to write. Writing has been my savior, giving me clarity, courage, and deeper acceptance. I cherish the writings of Greg, Sherry, and my mother, too, for their insights, love, and inspiration.

Last year, I began to offer a class. In *Write Your Own Story*, participants write to heal, to grow, to leave behind some of their experiences for loved ones.

Teaching a writing class has added a wonderful dimension to my relationship with Charlotte. Many times, I wanted her to help me write this book, but her academic writing is very different from memoir. She couldn't do it. I understood. The day she read my first completed draft she called and said, "Mom, I love it! Your writing has helped me heal." I cried. It was all I needed to hear her say. We had come full circle—supporting each other's efforts like we did in our early days of college.

I tell my students it doesn't matter who we write for, or what we write. Writing from the heart is what counts.

I stay active in Toastmasters. I am told my speeches on acceptance or finding the courage to change or the importance of writing are inspiring.

In service to the community, Larry and I launched a series of workshops at the local Senior Center where we encourage, teach, and help mature singles navigate the world of online dating, doing for others what Sherry did for me.

I will always continue to change and grow and accept what is behind me and look forward to what is ahead. Sherry said in her good-bye letter to me, "Please honor me by moving on and having a wonderfully happy life." I am.

Acknowledgments

Thank you, God. Without Your Guidance, I would have no story to tell. Thank you, Sherry and Greg, my angels. I will always love you. I miss you dearly.

Thank you, Sharla Nunes, for your perfect prayers that led me to open Greg's Bible, where I received the final sign that my story was ready to go.

Thank you to all my editors. I couldn't have done it without you. Jennie Nash, my invaluable book coach, you pushed me through to the end. Christine Pride, you are amazing. Dale Griffiths Stamos, it was a delight working with you. Larry Brooks, you taught me more about story structure than I could have ever imagined. Dr. Elizabeth McNeil, my first and last editor, thank you for all your red ink.

Thank you to Southern California Writer's Conference (SCWC) and the teachers who helped and supported me along the way: Laura Taylor; Judy Reeves; Maralys Wills; and Matt Pallamary.

Ingrid Ricks and Claudia Whitsitt, knowing you as authors and friends has inspired me to keep on writing. I admire you.

To all my "read and critique" writing buddies. Writers need each other. Believe me, I *really* needed you. Thank you for showing up in Encinitas, Oceanside, and Hidden Meadows.

Thank you to my beta readers: Joe Rice; Bob Norton; Jan Oliveira; Bev Campbell; Janet McLaughlin; and Tracy Wittrock Poulos.

At various stages along my writing journey, I shared my manuscript with many friends and neighbors. Some of you read it twice. Some of you read it aloud. Some of you printed it out and were fierce editors. I've decided to call you all my "earth angels." I held my breath while you read, one draft or another. Your beautiful and heartfelt responses helped me let go of my fears. Thank you. I love you all.

Thank you to my fellow Toastmasters for your incredible evaluations. You helped me grow as a speaker and a writer.

Thank you to all my Facebook friends for listening to me talk about my story.

Thank you to my writing students. You have given me so much. Please don't ever stop writing.

Thank you Shelley Schwartz and Melissa Harris, my dear longtime friends. You get it. I love you both. Thank you Ki Johnson, my new friend. Your love and support has been over the top.

Daphne Munro, your enthusiasm for my story and knowing that you have been such a great friend to Charlotte lights up my life. Thank you.

To my sisters, brother, nieces, nephews, and in-laws, thank you for loving and supporting me through my journey. I love you with all my heart.

Thank you, Lisa, Cam, Rose, Grace, and Laurel. Thank you, Gina, Ayrton, Avrey, and Myles. I love you all.

My dearest daughter, Dr. Charlotte Frambaugh-Kritzer, you were my first love. Thanks to you and Stuart for leading me down the right path.

Thank you, sweet Toby pup. During our one short year, you curled up beside me and made my writing better.

To my husband, Larry Curtis, thank you for cooking dinner and allowing me to be me. Thank you for changing my story—my life. My love for you is immeasurable.

About Rhonda

Rhonda Hayes Curtis is an award-winning speaker. The course she created, *Write Your Own Story,* inspires and teaches adults how to write from the heart. Her published story, *Meant to Be Together,* was selected by *Guideposts* magazine as one of the Top 10 Inspirational Stories of the year. She resides in Southern California with her husband, Larry Curtis.

Visit her website: RhondaHayesCurtis.com

31444687R10132

Made in the USA
San Bernardino, CA
10 March 2016